# ESSAYS ON VEDANTA AND WESTERN PHILOSOPHIES

# ESSAYS ON VEDANTA AND WESTERN PHILOSOPHIES

## (Vedanta as interpreted by Sri Aurobindo)

*Preface by Dr. Richard E. Aquila*

**Arun Chatterjee**

LOTUS PRESS

LOTUS PRESS
Box 325, Twin Lakes, WI 53181 USA
email:lotuspress@lotuspress.com
website: www.LotusPress.com

ISBN: 978-0-9406-7636-7

Library of Congress Number: 2017953130

Published by:

LOTUS PRESS

Lotus Press
P.O. Box 325
Twin Lakes, WI 53181 USA
800-824-6396 (toll free order phone)
262-889-8561 (office phone)
262-889-2461 (office fax)
www.lotuspress.com (website)
lotuspress@lotuspress.com (email)

Printed at Sri Aurobindo Ashram Press
Pondicherry
Printed in India

# Dedication

To my parents with Love and Adoration:
My mother: Late Kalyani Chatterji;
and
My father: Late Shyama Charan Chatterji

# Contents

## ABOUT AUTHORS

The author, Arun Chatterjee, is a Professor Emeritus of Civil and Environmental Engineering, The University of Tennessee, Knoxville, TN. He has been studying philosophy and religion for nearly 40 years. He has studied Sri Aurobindo's philosophy extensively. He published several articles on philosophy and religion in different journals in India. Some of those articles were revised and included in this book. (A more detailed background of him is presented in Author's Acknowledgement.)

The author of the Preface, Richard E. Aquila, is a Professor Emeritus of Philosophy, The University of Tennessee, Knoxville, TN. He is most known for his books and articles on Kant, but has also published numerous articles in leading journals on various figures in the history of philosophy and topics in the philosophy of mind. He is also a translator of Schopenhauer and co-editor of the Cambridge journal Kantian Review.

# Preface


**by Dr. Richard E. Aquila**

Professor of Philosophy at The University of Tennessee, USA


Some time before Arun Chatterjee and I retired from teaching at the University of Tennessee, I was honored by his request to attend my course on Jean-Paul Sartre's *Being and Nothingness.* A somewhat surprising request, I thought, from a Professor of Engineering. At the time, I supposed that it mainly expressed curiosity rooted in the fact that Arun's family was very well acquainted with Dr. J. N. Mohanty, the famous scholar of Husserlian phenomenology, and I was teaching Sartre with particular emphasis on his Husserlian background. It was only some time later, having developed an interest in the rather different world of Arthur Schopenhauer, and receiving a similar request from Arun, that I understood that the question of the nature of consciousness, as great thinkers have pursued it, was an independently powerful force for him. And so perhaps we can say that the present collection of essays bears witness to an ongoing process of liberation from the fascination of a study of the complexities of the realm of *prakriti* in favor of a turn to the mysteries of the realm of *purusha*. But of course too, perhaps these are not two "realms" but two sides of some single deeper reality. In any case, the present work bears witness to the antiquity and depth of this question in the philosophies and religions of India.

My own attention was drawn to Indian thought by Schopenhauer. But once having seen Chapter 13 of what it seems clear was Schopenhauer's initial encounter with Indian thought, the *Bhagavadgītā*[1] — and Schopenhauer in fact copied out parts of that chapter from the translation to which he had access at the time (1813) — I began to wonder to what still greater heights some of the greatest of western philosophers might have risen, had they made that same encounter.

1. See the essay by Urs App to which Dr.Chatterjee refers in his discussion of Schopenhauer.

To be sure, although there is much in the *Bhagavadgītā* to see as inspiration for Schopenhauer, he in fact cites it infrequently relative to his citation of the *Upanishads*. He clearly gives pride of place to the latter:

> But if [the reader] has even yet further [i.e. beyond a study of Plato and Kant] shared in the benefaction of the *Vedas*, access to which, opened up to us through the Upanishads, is in my eyes the preeminent greatness that this still young century has to show over earlier ones.... if, I thus assert, the reader has in fact already received and embraced consecration from the ages-old Indian wisdom, then he is best of all prepared to hear what I have to expound to him. It will then not speak to him, as to many others, in foreign, indeed hostile terms. For, if it does not sound too vain, I would maintain that every one of the individual and disparate pronouncements that constitute the Upanishads can be derived as a consequence from the thought to be communicated by me...[2]

In his published citations from the *Bhagavadgītā* Schopenhauer also fails to cite a striking passage that he took the trouble to copy from the translation (into German from an English translation) that he had studied in 1813, and that raises issues to which Dr. Chatterjee refers in his chapter on Schopenhauer, but which may be insufficiently explored generally in that context:

> Know Me as the Knower of the field in all fields, O Bharata (Arjuna). The knowledge of the field and its knower, do I regard as true knowledge.[3]

(In the translation read by Schopenhauer, the words translated — as is common to other translations — as "field" and "knower of

---

2. Arthur Schopenhauer, *The World as Will and Presentation*, Vol. One, tr. Richard E. Aquila and David Carus (New York: Pearson/Longman, 2008), preface to the first edition [1818], p. 13.

3. *The Bhagavadgītā*, tr. S. Radhakrishnan (London: George Allen & Unwin, 1948), Ch. 13.2.

the field" were left as transliterations of the Sanskrit: *Kshetra* and *Kshetra-gna.*) Here I would simply urge readers to follow Dr. Chatterjee's reference to the first chapter of the second volume (originally published in 1844, and frequently left unread by students of Schopenhauer's main work) of Schopenhauer's *The World as Will and Presentation*. Here the reader may not only be led to give more than customary consideration to the status of the Pure Subject in all cognizant subjects in Schopenhauer, as distinct from something called one Will in all portions of material reality. The reader may also be forced to consider the possibility that his first encounter with Indian philosophy left Schopenhauer with what was to become an internal struggle between, on the one hand, a dualism of Subject and Will, where the latter is viewed as a single force or drive expressing itself in all forces and drives within space and time, and on the other hand a dualism of a Pure Subject and a *field* of force or drive (as below, "Matter"), in itself not (quite) space or time, nor *in* space or time, but of such a character that, to the extent that it is apprehended within the forms of a subject's cognitive power, is *for* any cognizant subject the very space within which subjects differentiate objects (and are compelled to regard the inner being of those objects precisely as force or drive):

> Therefore crude, formless, completely dead (i.e. will-less) matter, which is not given in any experience, but presupposed in all, stands as a pure contrary opposite the cognizant subject, merely as such, which is likewise a presupposition of all experience. This subject is not in time; for time is just the more specific form belonging to all of its presentational activity. Matter, standing over against this subject, is, accordingly, eternal, imperishable, persists through all time, yet is not really extended, since extension gives form; thus it is not spatial. Everything else is in a state of constant arising and passing away...[4]

Perhaps long-standing recollection of the *Bhagavadgītā*'s "field"

4. Arthur Schopenhauer, *The World as Will and Presentation*, Vol. Two, tr. Richard E. Aquila and David Carus (New York: Pearson/Prentice-Hall, 2011), p. 17.

for all possible cognition, more fundamental than any objects discriminable *within* it, here returns to the surface for Schopenhauer, having been suppressed to large measure in favor of his fascination with the notion of a single *force* or *drive* expressing itself in all force or drive within objects. In any case, the reader of the present volume will be bound to surmise that some such struggle of competing visions was already long present within "the ages-old Indian wisdom" that inspired Schopenhauer.

I also venture some comment on another thinker with whom Dr. Chatterjee engages in this volume. In both Arthur Schopenhauer and the 17$^{th}$-century philosopher Baruch Spinoza, we encounter some version of monism. For both of these thinkers, all of the multiple particulars or events embraced within the whole of reality are but *one* reality in its self-expression as the *whole* of reality. But we encounter a tension within these monisms as well. In Schopenhauer, the tension is centered in the need to fathom the status of "subjectivity" in its relation to the single self-expressive reality. In Spinoza, the monism of a single self-expressive reality which all "other" things really *are* at bottom — which, to the consternation of the theists of his time and place, Spinoza called God (*deus*) — may seem in the first instance threatened from a very different direction, namely, from his argument for the conclusion that there must be infinitely many essential dimensions *of* that reality, dimensions of which what we know as *physical* reality would be but one example. These essential dimensions Spinoza called the *attributes* [Latin, *attributum*; pl. *attributa*] of his God. And he held that each of them is somehow "one" with that God — *and yet also*, each is in some way a self-expressive reality in its own right. This seems to be a tension unlike anything of the sort to be found in either Schopenhauer or the eastern thought with which he invites comparison. But there is also another fundamental tension in Spinoza.

As Spinoza puts it, one of the infinitely many attributes of his God is *cogitatio*: "thought," as most commonly translated into English, but perhaps better put as "cognizance." Yet it does not seem that *cogitatio* can really be on a par with the (other) attributes. According to Spinoza, each of the particulars or events that

God *is* in its self-expression — each of the "modes" of that divine "substance," in Spinoza's terminology — is to be regarded (as we might say, regarded in different "dimensions" of possible cognizance) as an expression of *each* of the attributes. To be sure, apart from the capacity for cognizance of cognizance itself, *human* cognizance is strictly limited to the *physical* mode of cognizance for Spinoza, thus to cognizance of the particular attribute thereby in question (which Spinoza, following Descartes, called *extensio*). But Spinoza also took it to follow, from the very nature of *cogitatio* as one of the attributes of God, not only that any mode of that divine "substance" — whatever else it might be (e.g. a bird in flight, as a mode of "extension") — must also be, in some dimension, itself a mode of *cognizance*; but beyond that, and precisely with respect to *all* that it might be beyond that (thus e.g. beyond being a bird in flight), it must be a mode of cognizance *of its very being as* whatever that is. From this it seems to follow that the "attribute" *cogitatio* has an infinitely farther reach than any of the other attributes, and in its unique way covers the whole field of being, in its own *single* being, that is covered by the particular ways of being of *all* of the other attributes. Thus again, out of the center of some kind of monism, a fundamental sort of dualism seems to arise — and a corresponding tension: on the one hand, a single field of being, more fundamental in its character than anything that could be captured by regarding it as either "physical" or otherwise; on the other hand, an all-encompassing "cognizance" thereof — which latter yet Spinoza himself calls a mere "attribute" of the former.

Needless to say, introducing the notion of an infinite "field," and some sort of infinite "cognizance" thereof, I take liberties which are not justified to the extent of my earlier comments regarding Schopenhauer and the *Kshetra* and *Kshetra-gna* of the *Bhagavadgītā*. Be that as it may, I simply conclude by calling attention to a pair of issues highlighted by Dr. Chaterjee in his chapter on Spinoza: first, there is the doctrine of a pervasive *conatus*, or *drive*, in Spinoza — surely in some way comparable to Schopenhauer's Will — which Spinoza sees as an aspect of *every* expression of *every* attribute within the infinite field of the divine being; and second, there is the fact that Spinoza seems to regard the attributes themselves as irreducibly distinct and fundamental "powers." In any case the question remains: where can all of this leave Spinoza's *cogitatio*? Wherever that might be, I assume that it is not far from the Pure Subject of Schopenhauer. Or from the Knower of the Field of "the ages-old Indian wisdom."

# Author's Acknowledgement

I could not have written this book without the help of many individuals. I did not study philosophy in a formal way. My professional background is civil engineering, and I taught at the University of Tennessee for many years. I grew up in a family of philosophy scholars and they included my father (Late Shyama Charan Chatterji), my maternal grandfather (Late Tarak Chandra Roy-Mukherjee), and my eldest sister, (Gopa Bhattacharya). I was familiar with the names of philosophers like Plato, Aristotle, Descartes, Kant, Shankara, Swami Vivekananda, and Sri Aurobindo. However, I became seriously interested in philosophy and religion after my father passed away in 1976. I began taking courses on different religions and philosophies at the University of Tennessee, Knoxville, where I was a Professor of Civil Engineering. As a professor at the university I could sit in the lectures of courses on philosophy and religious studies with the permission of the instructors. I came to know many professors in the Department of Religious Studies and also the Department of Philosophy. I was a member of the Board of Visitors of the Department of Religious Studies for several years. The professors to whom I am indebted for their help include: Late Dr. Jay Kim, Late Prof. Stan Lusby, Dr. James Fitzgerald, Dr. Gilya Schmidt of the Religious Studies Department; and Dr. Rem Edwards and Dr. Richard Aquila of the Philosophy Department. I want to thank Dr. Alan Nelson, Professor of Philosophy at the University of North Carolina at Chapel Hill. He helped me understand several concepts related to the philosophy of Spinoza. My sister Dr. Gopa Bhattacharya, who taught philosophy in India, answered numerous questions, which I asked her about philosophical concepts.

One interesting aspect of my learning experience is finding similarities of concepts and issues addressed by Indian and Western philosophies. Also interesting is how similar are the mystical versions of different religions. I have attempted to bring out these similarities in the various chapters of this book. Another experience, which I want to point out, is that I started my quest by first learning about religions, but gradually my interest deepened in the philosophical aspects more than common beliefs and practices of different religions. Learning about western philosophies helped me understand Indian philosophies more clearly. My primary interest now is in the philosophies of Sri Aurobindo, Swami Vivekananda, Vedanta, Arthur Schopenhauer, Baruch Spinoza, and Jean-Paul Sartre.

The inspiration for this book came from my father, who was a scholar of both eastern and western philosophies. He did not know when he was alive that I would pursue his interest earnestly. I also received strong encouragement for writing the book from my wife of 53 years, Kalpana, and also from my two daughters — Rinku and Ranee. I could not have completed the work without their cooperation and encouragement. I also appreciate the encouragement I received from my sister Dr. Mazumdar.

This acknowledgement will not be complete if I do not recognize the tremendous help from Dr. Richard Aquila. One of the greatest gifts of my life is my friendship with him whose expertise in philosophy is well known in the philosophy circle internationally. I was so happy when he agreed to write the Preface for the book. I was happier when he asked if he could review all the articles. He read each article word by word, and his comments and edits have enhanced the quality of this book tremendously.

Before closing I must point out that the original versions of all the chapters of the book were first published in different journals in India, and I am thankful to the editors of the journals for their permission to include them in this book. Considerable revisions have been made to all the articles, which make up different chapters. The journals and the articles are listed below:

1. Mother India, Published by Sri Aurobindo Ashram in Pondicherry, India: Chapters on (i) Reality and Self According to Vedanta as Explained by Sri Aurobindo; (ii) Schopenhauer and Indian Philosophies; (iii) Jewish Mysticism and Hinduism: A Comparison; and (iv) Place of Bhakti (Love and Adoration) in Sri Aurobindo's Yoga.

2. Prabuddha Bharata, Published by Advaita Ashrama (of Sri Ramakrishna Order), India: Chapters on (i) Religion, Philosophy, and Spirituality; (ii) God and World According to Spinoza and Ve-

danta; and (iii) Free Will and Determinism According to Vedanta and Western Philosophy.

3. Sraddha, Published by Sri Aurobindo Bhavan, Kolkata, India: (i) Philosophy of Immortality and Rebirth: Western and Eastern Views.

# Chapter 1

## Religion, Philosophy, and Spirituality

The terms religion, philosophy, and spirituality respectively are used by common persons in different ways, which are frequently not uniform. However, these terms have special meanings and implications which should be recognized, and the purpose of this chapter is to explain these meanings and implications. In the beginning of this article I will discuss some general concepts and issues related to these terms. Next I will examine the place of religion, philosophy, and spirituality in Hinduism.

### Religion, Philosophy, and Spirituality — History and Basic Concepts

Religions reflect man's desire to link himself with a Power or powers that he believes to be present beyond the phenomenal world, which is the world that we observe and experience with our senses and by scientific means. (I will use the word 'world' interchangeably with 'phenomenal world'.) The origin of religions can be traced to thousands of years BCE. Religion started in different forms such as animism, fetishism, and the deification of natural forces. [Animism believes in innumerable spiritual beings that are concerned with human affairs and capable of helping or harming human interests. Fetishism involves the religious worship of material objects alleged to be endowed with supernatural powers.] These approaches now are considered to be crude, but they reveal man's curiosity about something beyond the world. As time passed more refined concepts of God (and gods) gradually emerged, and different religions as we know them today originated in different parts of the world. Each of these religions is represented by certain beliefs about God and His relation with the universe and individual persons. These beliefs usually are found in certain books, which are considered to be sacred and used for guidance as to how a man is supposed to act in the world. These books also present concepts of how a person's actions in his present life would affect his life after death.

Most religions developed a hierarchy of organizations and clergies who have considerable influence on their followers as to how the respective religions are to be practiced. In some cases the clergy of a religion became dictatorial. The beliefs were imposed on the followers, and questions and discussions were not encouraged. In some cases the followers also became dogmatic and narrow minded instead of developing respect and tolerance for the views of other religions. The dogmas often make one think that only his religion contains truth and others do not. This kind of attitude helped develop animosity among different religions and led to atrocities and even many wars. However, it will be wrong to point out only the pitfalls of religions since they also have had considerable beneficial impact on societies. Even if a religion cannot do everything that it claims to be able to do, it can at least help a person uplift himself and develop higher morality and values. Faith in God also can help a person go through difficult circumstances of life.

There are many religions in the world, and among them are included the major religions known as Judaism, Hinduism, Buddhism, Taoism, Christianity, and Islam. The beginning of Judaism can be traced as far back as 2,000 BCE. The Vedas, which form the foundation of Hinduism, were written as early as 1,700 BCE. Buddhism (500 BCE) and Taoism (500 BCE) developed before the Common Era. Christianity and Islam began in about 30 CE and 600 CE respectively. The views held by these religions are not exactly alike, and there are also variations of belief and practice within each religion. One of the religions, viz., Buddhism, does not believe in God, and it has an exclusively existential orientation. Taoism also is not God oriented, and it focuses on a natural way of living. Judaism, Christianity, and Islam are strongly theistic. They also are dualistic in the sense that they consider God to be essentially different and separate from man. According to these religions man can approach God for help and salvation, and with the exception of their mystical forms, they believe that man can never unite with God. Hinduism, which I will discuss later in more detail, accommodates both theistic and non-theistic views. Hinduism has for the most part a monistic metaphysical view, which believes that everything is composed of one substance, although one school within it holds a pluralistic view.

Parallel with the development of religions other types of views emerged, and there was the beginning of philosophies. Whereas the religious beliefs are based more on faith and less on intellectual analysis, philosophies relied more on intellectual analysis and less on faith. Philosophies seek knowledge based on rational thinking. They encourage critical thinking. One major contribution of philosophies to society is that they questioned and removed many dogmas and superstitions that had roots in religions. The subject of philosophy includes a variety of topics such as Metaphysics, Epistemology, Philosophy of Mind (i.e., theories of self and consciousness), Ethics, and Philosophy of Religion.

Philosophies emerged independently in both the West and the East. In the West the Greek philosopher Socrates (469 — 399 BCE) is often considered to be the father of western philosophies. In the true spirit of philosophies he raised a variety of questions and was fond of arguing with others. He was followed by many brilliant philosophers such as (to mention some of those whom I will be discussing in this book) Plato (427 — 347 BCE), Aristotle (384 — 322 BCE), Ibn Rushd (1126 — 1198), Descartes (1596 — 1650), Spinoza (1632 — 1677), Kant (1724 — 1804), Schopenhauer (1788 1860), and Sartre (1905 — 1980). Many philosophers believed in God and some did not. Some were agnostic; and some were very materialistic and refused to speculate on anything beyond the phenomenal world. However, all western philosophers relied primarily on intellect. Many philosophies emerged also in the East. Hinduism and Buddhism have a strong philosophical component as they deal with philosophical issues such as Reality, Appearance, and Consciousness in a way that involves intellectual analysis. Most religious leaders in India were philosophers too. For example, Buddha and Shankaracharya (Shankara) were philosophers as well as religious persons. In India there are several schools of philosophy other than Hinduism and Buddhism. These include Nyaya, Vaisesika, Sankhya, Yoga, Mimamsa, Charvaka, and Jainism. In the Far

East Taoism (or, Daoism) and Confucianism developed at about the same time in China in the sixth century BCE. Taoism and Confucianism are not like traditional religions. Tao literally means the 'Way', and Taoism focuses on living harmoniously with Tao, which is a principle or force that is expressed in everything of the world; this is where the concept of 'yin and yang' originated. Confucianism played an important role in Chinese society. Its originator is Confucius (551 — 479 BCE), who is considered to be a sage. His philosophy deals with the right way to live and be faithful to one's relationship with others.

There is another area which is related to religions and also philosophies, and that is spirituality. The term 'spiritual' is used in different senses. For example, some persons think that the term spiritual is related to spirits that are forces of nature, or souls of dead persons; this is a narrow meaning of the term spirit. I will use the term spiritual in a broad sense according to which Spirit is the Ultimate Reality and is the essence or self of everything. So what is spirituality? According to Sri Aurobindo "spirituality is not a high intellectuality", and it also is not "religiosity or an ardent and exalted emotional fervour, and not even a compound of all these excellent things. Spirituality is in its essence an awakening to the inner reality of our being, to a spirit, self, soul which is other than mind, life and body, an inner aspiration to know, to feel, to be that, to enter into contact with the greater Reality beyond and pervading the universe which inhabits also our own being, to be in communion with It and union with It, ..." (LD p. 857)

A question can be raised if religion and spirituality are different and can be separated. Actually, most religions have both religious and spiritual components. A religion should be spiritual too, but it may not be practiced by many persons in a spiritual way. Spirituality does not have to be religious. As I discussed earlier, spirituality involves self-finding or self realization. A spiritual person, or at least a theistic one, believes that God dwells within his consciousness, and may also believe that he can reach Him through his inner self or soul without resorting to external rituals and practices of religions. One important aspect of spirituality is the feeling of oneness or unity with all entities of the world. Robert Solomon explained that "spirituality often takes the form of a generalized love of humanity and of all nature's creatures. Or it may take the form of a sense of oneness with the universe or togetherness with God." (Solomon, p. 49)

There is another aspect of religions, which is mysticism. (I have discussed mysticism in another chapter of the book.) There are some similarities between mysticism and spirituality. Spiritual, or (as often) mystical, personalities can be found in all religions. In Judaism Kabbalah represents a spiritual approach, and there are many teachers of Kabbalah who are highly spiritual persons. Within Christianity St. Teresa of Avila (1515 — 1582) and Pierre Teilhard de Chardin(1881 — 1955) are examples of highly spiritual persons. Within Islam Sufis are considered as spiritual persons of a mystic sort. One well known Persian poet who was a Sufi mystic is Rumi (1207 — 1273). In Hinduism there are several great persons who are philosophers as well as spiritual persons. (I will discuss Hindu spiritual personalities later.) Again, it is important to note that religious and spiritual approaches are not necessarily opposed to each other. Many saintly persons led religious as well as spiritual life. For example, Sri Ramakrishna (1836 - 1886), who is regarded in India as a great spiritual person and revered highly, used to perform religious rituals in a temple when he was young. However, as he gained the experience of Self and had numerous other spiritual experiences he stopped doing rituals. He was always united in his consciousness with his Mother Kali, a Goddess of Hindus.

I must point out that the blind followers of a religion who hold dogmatic views often commit atrocities against the followers of different religions. These practices have raised serious questions in many persons mind as to whether religions have lost their spiritual values. Swami Vivekananda talked about his hopes for establishing harmony among different religions and also for a universal religion. In a speech given at the World's Parliament of Religions held in Chicago, USA, in 1893, he said, "... but if there is ever to be a universal religion, it must be one which will hold no location in place or time; which will be infinite, like the God it will preach; and whose sun will shine upon the followers of Krishna and of Christ, on saints and sinners alike; which will not be the Brahminic or Buddhistic, Christian or Mohammedan, but the sum total of all these and still have infinite space for development; which in its Catholicity will embrace in its infinite arms and find a place for every human being [...] It will be a religion which will have no place for persecution or intolerance in its polity, which will recognize divinity in every man or woman, and whose whole scope, whose whole force, will be centered in aiding humanity to realize its own true, divine nature." (Swami Vivekananda, pp. 15-16) Unfortunately his ideal for a harmonious universal religion has not been realized yet.

**Place of Religion and Spirituality in Hinduism**

Hinduism is especially noteworthy for combining both religious and spiritual approaches. The original source-books of Hinduism are the Vedas. Yajur Veda, which is one of the four Vedas, has been very influential on Hindu religious practices, and it serves as the guidebook for priests for performing ceremonial rituals. The fundamental concept that underlies these rituals is that of sacrifice. External sacrifice involves offerings to gods in different forms. The offerings are of food, flowers, and, in rare cases, animals. It is important to note that these sacrifices are performed for gaining the favor of gods and not the Supreme Divine. Getting rewards such as wealth, fame, children, and protection from danger is the primary motive of these offerings. However, rituals in many cases are symbolic in nature and offerings can be interpreted as expressions of devotion and adoration for God. Rituals can be performed with correct knowledge and interpretation of the symbols with no expectation for rewards, and in that case they assume a spiritual nature.

The foundation of the spiritual approach of Hinduism is the Upanishads, which is referred to as Vedanta. Bhagavad Gita also is considered to be Vedantic literature. The Upanishads' spirituality involves the experience of Atman (Self), which represents consciousness at the highest level. According to the monistic view of Hinduism everything is composed of one substance, which is Self. For Hinduism spiritual practices lead to self-realization or finding one's true self. Self-realization is a difficult task and it requires a change or transformation of consciousness. One has to shift one's focus from the external ego to the inner self within. According to Katha Upanishad's Verse II. 1. 1., "The Self-existent pierced the openings (of the senses) outward; therefore, one looks outward and not at the self within. Occasionally a wise man, desiring immortality, turns his eyes inward and sees the self within him."

So what about Vedic rituals, which are practiced even today? Upanishads generally accept the validity and efficacy of Vedic rituals. However, they also point out that ceremonial sacrifices and ritualistic worship lead to gains that are materialistic and of limited value. Upanishads recommend a spiritual approach for gaining higher knowledge, finding the Self (Atman) and uniting with Brahman, the ultimate Reality. Among all of the Upanishads it is Mundaka Upanishad that addresses most clearly and directly the difference between ritualistic religious practice and spiritual approach toward God. Although Mundaka Upanishad does not denigrate Vedic rituals, it clearly presents spirituality as being superior to the ritualistic approach. I quote below a few verses from Mundaka, which present its view of the ritualistic approach.

Mundaka I. 2. 7: Frail indeed are the boats of these eighteen forms of sacrifice, which are said to be inferior karma. The fools who acclaim this as the highest good fall yet again into old age and death.

Mundaka I. 2. 10: These deluded men who regard sacrifices and works of merits as most important do not know any other good. Having enjoyed in the heaven won by good deeds, they enter again this world or a still lower one.

The following verses present the recommendations of Mundaka and Katha Upanishads for spiritual practice leading to self-realization, and this practice includes the study of Upanishads, gaining higher knowledge and equanimity, casting away of desires, and meditation on Brahman.

Mundaka II. 2. 3: Taking as the bow the great weapon of the Upanishads, place in it the arrow sharpened by meditation. Drawing it with a mind engaged in the contemplation of That (Brahman), O fair person, know that Imperishable (Brahman) as the target.

Katha II. 3. 14: When all desires that dwell within the heart are cast away, then a mortal becomes immortal, and he attains Brahman even here.

Bhagavad Gita's views on the ceremonial and ritualistic approach are similar to those of the Upanishads. Gita recognizes that the ritualistic approach can yield desired enjoyments and rewards, but these gains are of limited value. Gita prefers a psychological or spiritual approach. I present here a few verses that would reveal Gita's views on ceremonial sacrifices.

Chapter IX, Verses 20 and 21: The knowers of the three Vedas who drink the Soma juice and are cleansed of sin, worshipping Me with sacrifices, pray for the way to heaven. They reach the holy heavenly worlds and enjoy in heaven the pleasures of the gods. Having enjoyed the spacious world of heaven, they enter the world of mortals when their merit is exhausted. Thus conforming to the doctrine of the three Vedas, they, who are desirous of enjoyments, are subject to what comes and goes (birth and death).

Gita recognizes a variety of sacrifices, which can be performed. These sacrifices range from offerings of food and flowers, ascetic practices of self control, doing desireless work, and gaining knowledge of Brahman. After recognizing the validity of these sacrifices Gita reveals its preference for doing works as a sacrifice and also gaining knowledge as a sacrifice. In Verse IV — 33 of Gita it is said: "Sacrifice of knowledge, O Parantapa (Arjun), is greater than any material sacrifice. O Partha, all works without any exception culminate in wisdom." Gita presents its profound concept of sacrifice in Verse 24 of Chapter IV, which says: "Brahman is the offering, Brahman is the oblation, by Brahman it is poured into the fire of Brahman. Brahman is to be attained by one who is absorbed in the contemplation of the action of Brahman."

Sri Aurobindo explained the above presented Verse (IV — 24) as follows: "This then is the knowledge in which the liberated man has to do works of sacrifice. It is the knowledge declared of old in the great Vedantic utterances, 'I am He', 'All this verily is the Brahman, Brahman is this Self'. It is the knowledge of the entire unity; it is the One manifest as the doer and the deed and the object of works, knower and knowledge and the object of knowledge. The universal energy into which the action is poured is the Divine; the consecrated energy of the giving is the Divine; whatever is offered is only some form of the Divine; the giver of the offering is the Divine himself in man; the action, the work, the sacrifice is itself the Divine in movement, in activity; the goal to be reached by sacrifice is the Divine." (*Essays on the Gita*, p. 113)

Gita wants an aspirant of spirituality not only to understand the meaning of this verse, but also to act accordingly; and that requires him to be desireless and egoless. Every action, however small it may be, should be done for God as an offering, and this approach is expressed clearly in the following verse of Gita:

Chapter IX. 27. O son of Kunti (Arjuna), whatever you do, whatever you eat, whatever you offer as sacrifice, whatever you give, whatever austerities (Tapasya) you practice, (all) that you offer to Me.

**Closing Comments**

I would like to make two comments before I close this article. First, it seems to me that there is a growing trend toward spirituality as opposed to traditional religiosity among the younger generation today. This was expressed by Swami Satyamayananda in a recent article in which he wrote, "People are discovering that truth lies within and that the old running about in search of a guru or teacher is futile. One must be able to experiment with one's mind, and plunge inside, and discover truth. No method is standard and each one can tailor them according to their needs, time, and place." (Prabuddha Bharata, January 2015, pp. 60) This new trend represents the emergence of higher grades of consciousness and the development of the spiritual man about which Sri Aurobindo has written extensively in the book The Life Divine.

Second, traditionally spirituality has been somewhat otherworldly and has ignored the life on earth. Sri Aurobindo's vision is the establishment of spiritually transformed life on earth. It may take a long time for the complete realization of Sri Aurobindo's vision of a divine life on earth. However, it is clear that a new outlook of life and a new approach to spirituality are emerging among the new generation.

## References

Radhakrishnan, S., *The Principal Upanishads*, HarperCollins Publishers, India Pvt Ltd, 1994

Solomon, Robert C., *The Little Philosophy Book*, Oxford University Press, 2008

Sri Aurobindo, *The Life Divine*, Sri Aurobindo Ashram Trust, Pondicherry, India, 1970

Sri Aurobindo, *Essays on the Gita*, Eighth Edition, Sri Aurobindo Ashram Trust, Pondicherry, India, 1972

Swami Sarvananda, *Mundaka Upanishad*, Sri Ramakrishna Math, Mylapore, Chennai - 4, 2001

Swami Sarvananda, *Katha Upanishad*, Sri Ramakrishna Math, Mylapore, Chennai - 4, 2007

Swami Satyamayananda, "*The Spiritual Awakening of Humankind*", Prabuddha Bharata, Advaita Ashrama, Kolkata, India, January 2015, pp. 46-50.

Swami Vivekananda, *Selections from Swami Vivekananda*, Advaita Ashram, Calcutta (Kolkata), Fifth Edition, 1970

# Chapter 2

# Reality and Self According to Vedanta as Explained by Sri Aurobindo

## Introduction

Philosophical issues such as reality versus appearance, permanence versus change, and self versus not-self, have been examined by eastern and western philosophers as far back as the sages of Upanishads (700 BCE) in the East and Plato (400 BCE) in the West. In this article I will examine issues involving reality and appearance, and I will present the views of Vedanta philosophy on the concepts of Ultimate Reality and its expression as the Self of the universe and self of individual entities. Thus I will examine the concept of universal Self as well as that of individual selves. I will capitalize Self when referring to its universal status; and I will not capitalize self when referring to its individual status.

Vedanta is very prominent among the Hindu schools of philosophy. There have been different interpretations of Vedanta by a few great scholars of old time, and there are different schools of Vedanta based on their interpretations. Scholars of modern time also have their own view, and one of them is Sri Aurobindo. I will present brief discussion about the philosophy of three major schools within Vedanta with regard to Reality and Self. I will also add Sri Aurobindo's interpretation of Vedanta on this subject.

## Ultimate Reality and Reality of the World

Vedanta philosophies are based on three canonical works (*Prasthana-Traya*), which are Upanishads, Brahma Sutras, and Bhagavad Gita (or Gita). The Upanishads are the original source of Vedanta, which literally means "end of Vedas". The teachings of Upanishads were presented in a systematic manner in Brahma Sutras by sage Badarayana. The Brahma Sutras are also referred to as Vedanta Sutras. The sutras or verses of Brahma Sutras are very short and difficult to interpret. Several scholars of antiquity interpreted these sutras, and prominent among them are Shankaracharya (788 — 820 CE), Ramanujarcharya (1055 — 1137 CE), and Madhvacharya (1299 — 1378 CE). I will refer to these three scholars as Shankara, Ramanuja and Madhva respectively. There are several other scholars of yore who also have given their own interpretation of Vedanta. I will discuss only the views of Shankara, Ramanuja, and Madhva, which led to the development of the three major schools of Vedanta philosophy — Adwaita (Nondualism) of Shankara, Visishta Adwaita (Nondualism of Qualified Brahman) of Ramanuja, and Dwaita (Dualism) of Madhva. The views of these scholars differ although their views are based on the same sources of Vedanta literature. Adwaita and Visishta Adwaita represent 'monism' (or 'nondualism') since one of its fundamental tenets is that there is a single principle that forms the reality of everything, or in other words this single principle is the essence of everything of the phenomenal world (or, world), and also everything that is beyond the world. (Phenomenal world is the world as it presents itself to the senses, and also to any scientific way of thinking with its *foundation* in what presents itself to the senses.) This single principle is Brahman. The metaphysical concept of Dwaita Vedanta is very different from the other two major schools. Although the word 'dwaita' means 'dual' this school believes in pluralism as it believes that every entity of the world has its own unique substance or essence.

All schools of Vedanta recognize that the 'Ultimate Reality', or Supreme Reality, which is the source of the world, is Brahman, which is self-existent, independent, immutable, and beyond causality. However, there is disagreement among these schools over a few issues, such as: (a) does Brahman have qualities (*Saguna*), or is it quality-less (*Nirguna*); (b) does it have personality, or is it impersonal; (c) are the world and individual selves truly real or illusory? I will examine these issues one by one.

In Shankara's metaphysical scheme Brahman is devoid of qualities and it is also impersonal. It is undifferentiated pure consciousness; it transcends the world and is beyond space and time. Shankara's view that Brahman is devoid of qualities and do not have a personal aspect is somewhat problematic. In Vedantic literature Brahman with qualities and personality is God, or Ishwara, and He is considered to be the creator and sustainer, *i.e.*, Lord, of the world. For example, in Bhagavad Gita Ishwara is presented as a friend who provides spiritual shelter to His devotees. However, according to Shankara quality-less and impersonal Brahman alone is truly real and he called this reality the supreme reality (*Paramarthika Satta*). In his view Ishwara and the world are the appearance (*Vivarta*) of Brahman, and this appearance is caused by Maya, which is an inscrutable power of Brahman. However, he acknowledged that as long as a person remains in ignorance Ishwara and the world appear to be real, and he called this reality the practical reality (*Vyavaharika Satta*). In Shankara's view when knowledge is gained and ignorance is removed the reality of God (Ishwara) and the world is sublated. He used an example of a coiled rope, which is mistaken by a person to be a snake in the dark. When light is shed on the snake, the person realizes that the snake is not real and the true identity of the coiled rope is revealed. Similarly when ignorance is removed and true knowledge is gained a person realizes that what appears to be the world is not real and that the true Reality is Brahman. Shankara also did not acknowledge the true reality of individual selves. Evidently Shankara could not accept the concept that immutable and indivisible Brahman can transform itself to form the mutable world with multiple selves and still remain unchanged in its original state; his philosophy avoided this apparent contradiction by denying that the phenomenal world with multiplicity is truly real. It should be pointed out that Shankara's view raises a few questions one of which is: Why would Brahman manifest an unreal world in which fictitious selves would get entangled in ignorance only to seek release from the illusory world? The example of a rope and a snake also raises the question: how can a person have the idea that the coiled rope is a snake unless he has experienced a real snake somewhere else?

According to Ramanuja there cannot be any undifferentiated and impersonal Reality, and he rejected Shankara's philosophy of impersonal Brahman without any quality. For him the Ultimate Reality is Brahman with personality and qualities. Personal Brahman with qualities is Ishwara or God with whom one can establish a relationship. Ramanuja believed that the manifested world is truly real and is the transformation (*Parinama*) of Brahman. However, this transformation does not affect the original state of Brahman. According to him Ishwara, matter, and souls form a unity, but matter and souls exist as the body of Ishwara. Thus Ramanuja's nondualism recognizes a kind of identity of matter and souls with God, but according to him matter and souls cannot become God. This concept is known as identity with a difference. His philosophy is called Visishtadvaita, which often is translated as Qualified Nondualism. According to Ramanuja Brahman is nondual and yet it is qualified by the world, which includes matter and individual souls. Ramanuja believed that matter and souls are real, eternal, and are inseparable from God. They are one with God with regard to their essence or substance, but as modes (*Prakara*) of the spiritual substance of God, they are different from God.

Madhva's concept of Ultimate Reality has similarities with that of Ramanuja. Both of them rejected the concept of impersonal and attribute-less Brahman, and they believed in Brahman who has personality; but there is a fundamental difference between their philosophies. Ramanuja believed that despite the fact that matter and individual souls are different from God they are modes (*Prakara*) of God's spiritual substance and are inseparable from Him. Madhva was a pluralist. As I commented earlier that although his philosophy is called 'dwaita' (Vedanta), which means 'dualism', he actually believed in pluralism according to which every entity of the world has its own unique substance or essence. Thus the world of matter and souls are made of substances which are different from that of God (and also from each other), and they are eternally separate from Him.

Sri Aurobindo's views on Ultimate Reality, manifested world, and individual souls are based primarily on his interpretation of Upanishads and Bhagavad Gita, but his views do not match exactly with those of the great scholars of the past. He believed in nondualism, or monism, but his views are more comprehensive than those of Shankara and Ramanuja. According to him Brahman is both *Saguna* and *Nirguna*, i.e., it has qualities and at the same it is without qualities. Similarly Brahman is personal as well as impersonal. These characteristics are aspects of the same Brahman, and one of these does not cancel the other. These different aspects complement each other. His view is supported by Upanishads and Gita, and many other scholars also agree with this view. For example, in Svetasvatara Upanishad, Verses VI — 2 and VI — 16 describe God as *Guni*, possessor of qualities whereas Verse VI — 11 describes Him as *Nirguna*, devoid of qualities. Sri Aurobindo believed that the logic that we use to analyze matters and issues of the finite world cannot be applied to Brahman, which is infinite. In the Upanishads there are several examples of apparently contradictory characteristics of Brahman. For example, Verse 5 of Isha Upanishad says: "That moves and That moves not; That is far and the same is near; That is within all this and that also is outside all this." These statements appear to be contradictory, but the Upanishad uses these to indicate the limitations of human intellect, which cannot fully conceive of the Absolute, which is infinite. Human intellect tries to apply the laws of the finite world to the Absolute, Brahman, and it fails to grasp the freedom of Brahman to have a stable status with latent qualities outside space and time and at the same time express those qualities in movement in space and time without disturbing its stability. Sri Aurobindo commented that "The Infinite is illimitably free, free to determine itself infinitely, free from all restraining effect of its own creations." (LD, p. 333)

Sri Aurobindo did not accept Shankara's interpretation of *Maya* as the power that creates illusion. He also rejected Shankara's view that the world and individual selves are not truly real. His concept of nondualism (monism) accepts both the reality of Brahman and the reality of the world. In his words: "The real Monism, the true Adwaita, is that which admits all things as the one Brahman and does not seek to bisect Its existence into two incompatible entities, an eternal Truth and an eternal Falsehood, Brahman and not-Brahman, Self and not-self, a real self and an unreal and yet perpetual Maya. If it be true that the Self alone exists, it must be also true that all is the Self." (LD, p. 31) He further added that "If the Reality alone exists and all is Reality, the world also cannot be excluded from that Reality; the universe is real. If it does not reveal to us in its forms and powers the Reality that it is, if it seems only a persistent and yet changing movement in Space and Time, this must not be because it is unreal or because it is not at all That, but because it is a progressive self-expression, a manifestation, an evolving self-development of That in Time which our consciousness cannot yet see in its total or its essential significance. (LD, pp. 464-465).

Sri Aurobindo criticized the two extreme views of materialists and spiritualists. The extreme form of materialism believes only in the phenomenal world and experiences of sensual perception, and it denies Spirit. The extreme form of spiritualism believes only in Spirit and denies the material world. He observed that spiritualistic view was dominant in India for a long time in the past and it led to asceticism and a life-shunning attitude. He also commented that materialistic views and scientific findings, although they have limitations, helped clear out many superstitious beliefs of Indian society. Sri Aurobindo believed that Reality includes both spirit and matter and it has a static as well as a dynamic aspect — Being and Becoming. In Sri Aurobindo's metaphysical scheme there is a gradation, or strata, of existence. At the summit, or highest level, is Brahman, which is the 'Ultimate Reality', the Absolute. At the other end is material existence. In between these two extremes there are many other strata or planes of existence.

Sri Aurobindo accepts the concept that Brahman manifests itself as the phenomenal world using its consciousness-force (Chit-Shakti), which is *Maya*. Maya is referred to as the self-power of Brahman, *devatma-shakti*, in Shvetashwatara Upanishad (Verse I. 3). For manifestation Brahman takes the posture of unchanging Atman (Self) and emanates itself as the changing phenomenal world. The view that the world is a real expression of the Brahman and is constituted by its substance or essence is fully supported by the Upanishads and Bhagavad Gita. A great saying (*Mahavakya*) of Upanishads is "*Sarvam Khalu Idam Brahman*" (Verse III.14.1 of Chandogya), which means "All this verily is Brahman". There are verses in other Upanishads also that recognize that the world is a real manifestation of Brahman. In Sri Aurobindo's view the manifested world does not diminish or change Brahman in any manner. The verse that is used as the Invocation in Isha Upanishad says: "That is full, this is full. The full comes out of the full. Taking the full from the full the full itself remains." This statement contradicts mathematical principles that we normally use. However, what the Upanishad is conveying is that mathematical principles of finite world are not applicable to Brahman, and that the manifestation of the world does not in any manner affect the integrity of Brahman. Sri Aurobindo commented that the verse represents "the mathematics of the Infinite". (LD, p. 339)

It should be noted that the philosophy of Vedanta is based not only on intellectual analysis but also on intuitive spiritual experience of great persons. Sri Aurobindo believed that the differences in the views of Shankara, Ramanuja, and Madhva as to the nature of Ultimate Reality and also of the reality of individual selves can be reconciled. From his own spiritual experience he found that there is a truth behind the different views of Shankara, Ramanuja, and Madhva. He attributed the differences in their views to the spiritual experience of each, which focused on a specific aspect of Reality and missed the more comprehensive experience.

**Statuses of Self according to Vedanta**

In the process of self-manifestation Brahman expresses itself in a variety of manners or modes, and assumes different postures or statuses. Sri Aurobindo wrote about a graded series of existence. Brahman is present at each of the levels as Self (Atman). At the highest level of manifestation Brahman is Supreme Self (Paramatman), which is transcendent with respect to the universe. The Su preme Self takes the posture of Self (Atman) for the purpose of manifestation, and Self is universal, or cosmic, in nature. Moreover, the universal Self (Atman) has an individual status (jivatman) as well. It is important to note that these statuses and modes exist simultaneously and they are intimately connected. The process of manifestation creates certain apparent dualities, which are difficult to reconcile. For example, one may wonder how the transcendent Supreme Self can also be the universal Self without giving up its transcendent status, or how can one Brahman become many existences of the universe without giving up its unity. Further, how can Self be immutable when its manifested forms are mutable, and how can it be impersonal and also personal? Sri Aurobindo repeatedly pointed out that the ordinary logic used for analyzing the matters of phenomenal world is not applicable to Brahman or Self, which is beyond space and time. One needs to rely on intuitive knowledge for comprehending these issues and concepts.

As presented above, there are three statuses of Self, which are transcendent, universal, and individual. I will examine the three statuses briefly in this section, and later examine in detail various aspects of an individual self.

### Transcendent Supreme Self (Paramatman)

At its highest status Self transcends the phenomenal world and is called the Supreme Self, Paramatman. Paramatman is the highest posture of Brahman with regard to the manifested world. It is the origin of the spiritual substance of all forces and forms of the universe; however, at this supra-cosmic stage it has not extended itself in time and space. It is timeless and spaceless. The world is a projection or an emanation of the Supreme Self, and individual beings of the universe also are emanations of Supreme Self.

### Universal Self (Atman)

Universal Self is the self-extended mode of the transcendent Supreme Self (Paramatman) for the purpose of its manifestation. Universal Self has two aspects — static and dynamic. The static aspect is immutable and transcends the universe whereas the dynamic aspect is immanent in the world as the inner essence of Nature (Prakriti), which is out in front and visible as the mutable world. Universal Self contains and supports all things and forms of the manifested world in its being, but it is not bound by any of them. It is the omnipresent Reality of the manifested world. Self, i.e., Universal self, itself is not subject to time and space, but it supports time and space of the manifested world as figures of its consciousness. Sri Aurobindo repeatedly pointed out that according to Vedanta Self is in all things, all things are in Self, and all things are becomings of Self.

There is a famous series of verses in Chandogya Upanishad, which describe how the sage Uddalaka Aruni taught his son Svetaketu the concept of Self. He used a variety of examples of material and living things of the world and declared that the subtle essence of all these is the Self or Atman. One of these verses, which is repeated several times, is as follows:

> Verse VI. 8. 7. That which is the subtle essence, this whole world has for its Self. That is the true. That is the Self. That thou art, Svetaketu.

For Adwaita (Nondualistic) Vedanta of Shankara the realization of the impersonal static and silent universal Self is the straight way to individual liberation (Mukti). Sri Aurobindo pointed out that an exclusive focus on the experience of static and silent universal Self can make the phenomenal world appear to be unreal, and this experience can lead to a negative approach to life and a life-shunning philosophy. Sri Aurobindo did not ignore the significance of silent Self. In his view the experience of silent Self is important and essential for a spiritual practitioner, but there also is a dynamic mode of Self and that too must be experienced in order to get a complete understanding of Reality.

The dynamic mode of Universal Self is referred to in Gita as the mutable Self, i.e., Kshara Purusha. When Self manifests itself it reveals its two aspects — Prakriti (i.e., Nature) and Purusha (Conscious Being). Purusha and Prakriti are not separate principles and they are intimately connected. Prakriti is the manifestation of the power of Purusha, and in the phenomenal world it is out in front with Purusha hidden in it. The phenomenal world, i.e., Nature, is in 'time and space' and everything in it changes. However, the mutable forms of all objects and creatures of the phenomenal world, which Nature creates, are not empty forms. Self as Purusha dwells in all forms as their substance. Nature is active and mutable, and the Purusha hidden in it reflects the mutations and movement of Nature. So this Purusha in Nature appears to be mutable, or Kshara, but the Purusha in its essence is not mutable. Sri Aurobindo explained in the Essays on the Gita (p. 423) that the mobility of mutable (Kshara) Purusha occurs in the immobility or stability of immutable (Akshara) Purusha, which is Universal Self. In his words, "These two then are the two spirits we see in the world; one emerges in front in its action, the other remains behind it steadfast in that perpetual silence from which the action comes and in which all actions cease and disappear into timeless being, Nirvana." (EG, p. 423) I should point out that the experience of universal Self and/or Universal Purusha — makes one realize the oneness, or unity, of all individual selves and entities.

Individual Self (Jivatman)

The topic of individual self is of great interest not only to philosophers but also to common persons. To an individual person his possessing a self of his own seems obvious and certain. However, the reality of an individual self has been debated for a long time in Indian philosophies as well as in western philosophy. There are several philosophical issues and questions related to individual selves, which are addressed in eastern and western philosophies. In the following section I will present the Vedantic view of an individual self as expounded by Shankara, Ramanuja, and Madhva along with Sri Aurobindo's view. Lastly I will present a few concepts of an individual self that represent Sri Aurobindo's contribution to Vedanta philosophy.

## Individual Self

Individuals experience their selves in different ways depending on the level of their spiritual development. Commonly an individual identifies himself with his ego. With spiritual experience he can experience his individual self as an individual purusha and/or as jivatman. An individual purusha is a conscious being or a person separate from ego but intimately connected to Prakriti (Nature). Jivatman is an individual's unchanging self and outside Prakriti. I will discuss these concepts in the following sections.

Ego (Ahamkara)

The most common experience of an individual self is that of ego (Ahamkara). At the level of ego one feels that he is separate from others, and he does not have a sense of unity with others except perhaps with very near relatives. There is almost unanimous agreement among Indian philosophers that ego is a temporary construction of Nature (Prakriti) and that it does not represent one's authentic or true self. However, ego serves a useful purpose. Sri Aurobindo pointed out that the sense of individuality created by ego helps to centralize a person's experiences. In his own words: "The formation of a mental and vital ego tied to the body-sense was the first great labour of the cosmic Life in its progressive evolution; for this was the means it found for creating out of matter a conscious individual." (SY, p. 341) Sri Aurobindo also emphasized that ego must be discarded for spiritual advancement. In his own words: "The dissolution of this limiting ego is the one condition, the necessary means for this very cosmic Life to arrive at its divine fruition: for only so can the conscious individual find either his transcendent self or his true Person." (SY, p. 341) Gita repeatedly pointed out that one's ego is the primary cause of his suffering. According to Verse II. 71 of Gita one who acts without the sense of 'my-ness' (Nirmama) and 'I-ness' (Nirahamkara) attains peace.

Now the question that naturally arises is: if ego and ego-sense are not our true self, what is truly our individual self? The terms that are most widely used in Indian philosophy for an individual's true self are 'jivatman', and 'purusha'. These are different postures of the same entity and there are some differences. I will discuss each of these one by one.

Jivatman (Jiva)

In everyday language of common persons jiva refers to any living being. In Indian philosophy the term jiva is used to mean an individual spiritual self or jivatman. However, there is disagreement among different schools of thought within Hindu philosophy as to what exactly a jiva is composed of. According to some writers jiva is the physical and psychological complex that we commonly think we are. This complex is made up of a gross physical body also called food sheath, and a subtle body made up of vital and mental sheaths. (Some writers include with these another body called causal body, or '*Karana Sarira*'.) Some others think that jiva includes only the subtle body of vital and mental sheaths. According to these definitions jiva is made up of elements of Prakriti (Nature) and thus is not a spiritual entity. However, most scholars of Vedanta agree that jiva is a spiritual entity and resides outside space and time. Prominent scholars of Vedanta differ in their views regarding the status of a jiva as to whether it is eternal or temporary, real or illusory.

With regard to an individual self Shankara's view is similar to his view of Ishwara and the phenomenal world. He granted only practical reality to individual selves and he believed that individual selves are neither truly real nor eternal. According to him it is due to ignorance (*Avidya*) that an individual person identifies himself with his ego formed by the psycho-physical organism and thinks that he is separate from Brahman and also other individuals. When his ignorance is removed his sense of individuality disappears, and he realizes his identity, or non-duality, with universal Self (Atman), which is Brahman. Then he is liberated. This realization can occur even when one is alive, and at this status he is called *jivan-mukta*, which means 'free while alive'. Final freedom is gained after leaving one's body. Shankara's philosophy does not reconcile the difference between the multiplicity of the world and Brahman.

Ramanuja's view on individual souls is compatible with that of Bhagavad Gita, which is expressed in Verse 15 — 7, which says, "It is an eternal portion of Me that becomes the jiva in a world of jivas." Sri Aurobindo recognized this compatibility and made the following comment: "It is evidently this idea of an eternal individual which leads the Gita to avoid any expression at all suggestive of a complete dissolution, *laya*, and to speak rather of the highest state of the soul as a dwelling in Purushottama, *nivasisyasi mayyeva*. If, when speaking of the one Self of all, it seems to use the language of Adwaita, yet this enduring truth of the eternal individual, *māmamśah sanātanah (an eternal portion of me)*, adds something which brings in a qualification and appears almost to accept the seeing of the Visishtadwaita, ..." (Essays on the Gita, p. 431, 1972) According to Ramanuja by appropriate spiritual practice, which includes contemplation of God with *bhakti* (love and devotion) and self-surrender, a self can have a vision of God and be liberated from the cycle of birth and death (*Samsara*) after his body perishes. However, his individuality persists and he lives in the abode of God, which is called *Vaikuntha*, where he enjoys eternal peace and happiness in the presence of God. Madhva also believed that although matter and selves are separate from God they are entirely dependent on Him. According to Madhva individual selves are eternal, and no two selves are alike. Liberated selves maintain their individuality.

Sri Aurobindo believes in the reality and eternal status of an individual self. He frequently refers to Gita's verse XV- 7, which says, "It is verily an eternal portion of Me that becomes the Jiva (living being) in the world of Jivas (living beings) and cultivates the six senses, including mind, which abide in Nature." Referring to this verse Sri Aurobindo wrote in Essays on the Gita: "This is an epithet, a statement of immense bearing and consequence. For it means that each soul, each being in its spiritual reality is the very Divine, however partial its actual manifestation of him in Nature. And it means too, if words have any sense, that each manifesting spirit, each of the many, is an eternal individual, an eternal unborn undying power of the one Existence. We call this manifesting spirit the Jiva, because it appears here as if a living creature in a world of living creatures, and we speak of this spirit in man as the human soul and think of it in the terms of humanity only." (EG, p. 430-431)

It is important to note that jivatman is not a mutable entity as it is outside Nature (Prakriti), which constitutes the phenomenal world in time and space. Jivatman is immutable (Akshara). It is a pure subject and witness. It is spirit and superior to Nature. Jivat man is a portion of the Supreme Self in the sense that it is a partial manifestation of it. According to Gita's Verse II -20, "It is not born, nor does it die at any time; nor having once come into being it will not come into being again." A jiva is a centre of the universal Self (Atman). In Sri Aurobindo's view Self is multiple in jivas. Jivatman is at once individual and universal. It feels its oneness with universal Self (Atman) and Supreme Self (Paramatman), and it also feels oneness with other jivatmans while maintaining its own individuality. Sri Aurobindo explained: "It [each jivatman] is one, yet different [from other Jivatmas]. . . . Essentially one Jiva has the same nature as all — but in manifestation each puts forth its own line of Swabhava". (LY, Part 1, p. 280) Swabhava of an individual is his unique and true inner nature, which seeks expression in life. In Sri Aurobindo's words, "in nature each of us has a principle and will of our own becoming." (EG, p. 502) Jivatman is the true individual self, the true person, and it presides over the development of an individual being in Nature from behind or above. It may be added that the experience of jivatman by an individual is gained only at a high level of spiritual development.

Individual Purusha (Soul or Conscious Being)

In a previous section in which I discussed universal Self (Atman) I pointed out that Gita recognizes two statuses of Self, which are immutable (Akshara) and mutable (Kshara). The immutable universal Self or Universal Purusha is outside time and space although it supports the phenomenal world, which is in time and space. The mutable Purusha is hidden in Prakriti (Nature), which is the phenomenal world. These two statuses of universal Self are also applicable in the case of an individual self. Jivatman is the immutable individual self above or outside Nature, and purusha is the individual conscious being, or soul, that participates in the mutations of Nature (Prakriti). I mentioned earlier that when Self manifests itself it reveals its two aspects — Prakriti (i.e., Nature) and Purusha (i.e., Conscious Being). This is true for an individual self also. An individual purusha is always present with its Prakriti, and it is the person to whom the personality belongs. Individual purusha supports the outer personality from behind. It should be noted that the outer personality of an individual purusha changes, but the purusha in itself does not change.

For each individual person there is one central purusha, and as Sri Aurobindo points out "it adapts itself to the formations of Nature". (LD, p. 896) This view is in agreement with that of Taittiriya Upanishad, which recognizes different purushas corresponding to different grades of an individual's Nature. Taittiriya Upanishad refers to these different purushas in Verses 2, 3, 4, and 5 of Section II. In the physical body of an individual person there is a purusha, which is called physical self or purusha (annamaya atma). Similarly, there is a vital purusha (pranamaya atma) and there is also a mental purusha (manomaya atma). The central purusha at the core of one's being is referred to by different expressions in the Upanishads. In Verses III. 7. 3 to 23 of Brhadaranyaka it is called inner controller or ruler (atmantaryami). In Verse III. 14. 4 of Chandogya it is called the self within the heart (atmantar hridaye). Shvetashvatara refers to this as the person who is the inner self (purusha antaratma) in Verse III. 13. In Maitri it is called the elemental self (bhutatma) in Verse III. 2. I will discuss more about the nature and role of individual purushas in Sri Aurobindo's philosophy in the following section.

**Individual Self and Soul in Sri Aurobindo's Philosophy**

Sri Aurobindo agreed with the general concepts of Vedanta regarding the statuses of Self, which are Supreme Self (Paramatman), universal Self (Atman) and individual self (jivatman). However, he disagreed with the views of certain schools of Vedanta, which do not accept individual selves as eternal and real. He strongly rejected the extreme form of Adwaita Vedanta known as Mayavada, which believes that the manifested world and its inhabitants are illusory. His philosophy goes beyond traditional Vedantic thought as it affirms an evolution of consciousness and a recovery of self-awareness in which an individual self, or soul, plays a very important role. In his own words, "It is through the conscious individual being that this recovery [of consciousness] is possible; it is in him that the evolving consciousness becomes organized and capable of awaking to its own Reality. The immense importance of the individual being, which increases as he rises in the scale, is the most remarkable and significant fact of a universe which started without consciousness and without individuality in an undifferentiated Nescience. This importance can only be justified if the Self as individual is no less real than the Self as cosmic Being or Spirit and both are powers of the Eternal." (LD, p. 755) I already pointed out that Sri Aurobindo did not accept the view of some scholars of Vedanta who believe that when an individual attains enlightenment and goes beyond the consciousness of separative individuality, he merges with the universal Self and loses his individuality. According to Sri Aurobindo a person can experience the universality of his self and its individuality simultaneously.

Recognizing the importance of an individual being in his philosophy let us examine what Sri Aurobindo considers to be the true self or soul of an individual person. We have already stated that Sri Aurobindo repeatedly pointed out that the ego personality of a human being is not his true self, and he is in full agreement with traditional Hindu philosophy on this issue. He also pointed out that ego serves a useful purpose in organizing and centralizing a person's experience of life. According to Sri Aurobindo there is a real spiritual individual behind a person's outer personality. This spiritual individual has two statuses. One of these statuses is that of 'jiva' or 'jivatman', which is outside space and time and is not in mutable Nature. The other status is that of individual purusha (or individual conscious being), which is in Nature and supports an individual person's Prakriti (Nature).

An individual's nature has several components or elements such as the physical body, vital energy, and mind. All these instrumental elements or powers are supported by corresponding purushas about which I wrote earlier. Sri Aurobindo points out that in addition to the instrumental elements there is a divine element in every person, which is its central purusha or soul in the embodied life. Jivatman is the true central being, but it is outside space and time and is represented in Nature by what Sri Aurobindo calls psychic entity or soul. In his own words "the soul, representative of the central being, is a spark of the Divine supporting all individual existence in Nature." (LY, Part 1, p. 267)

The psychic entity is the soul in essence and it is undifferentiated Divine consciousness. The psychic entity or soul gains a variety of experience from repeated births, and it attains individuality in human beings. The individuality or personality of psychic entity is what Sri Aurobindo calls 'psychic being', or Chaitya Purusha. A psychic being resides in the spiritual heart of a person and secretly participates in his life and continues to evolve. It is the inmost of all purushas in Nature and it secretly supports the other purushas — mental, vital and physical purushas . Psychic being plays a very important role in Sri Aurobindo's integral yoga. In Sri Aurobindo's words a psychic being "is a flame born out of the Divine and, luminous inhabitant of the Ignorance, and grows in it till it is able to turn it towards the Knowledge." (LD, p. 225) Psychic being is full of love and devotion for the Divine or God.

Sri Aurobindo explained in detail the differences between psychic entity (or soul), psychic being, and jivatman in the Letters on Yoga and also in The Life Divine. In brief, jivatman is above the manifested life and it presides over the evolution of psychic being and other purushas, but it itself is unborn and does not change. A psychic being is the personality of the psychic entity (i.e., psychic essence) of an individual person, and it is the primary representative of jivatman in terrestrial life. Whereas jivatman is the true central being of a person, the psychic being acts as the central being in the person's embodied life. Jivatman comes into being during the descending movement of the Supreme Self (Paramatman) leading to the manifestation of the phenomenal world. It is prior to the ascending movement of consciousness from matter. On the other hand a psychic being is formed in the ascending or evolutionary process and it is mutable, but it is immortal. After a person dies his psychic being goes to the psychic world where it assimilates past life's experience, and then it returns to terrestrial life and enters a new body at its birth for more experience and growth.

I mentioned earlier that Sri Aurobindo calls psychic being the purusha in the heart or 'Chaitya Purusha'. This particular expression, however, is not used anywhere in either Upanishads or Gita. Gita refers to an individual self as jiva (or jivatman), and also as *Ksetrajna* or knower of the field, which is purusha. However, there is nothing mentioned in Gita that corresponds exactly to psychic being. There are a few verses in Upanishads that refer to an embodied purusha (soul), which is similar in concept to a psychic being. I referred earlier to a few verses from different Upanishads that mention an inner and central self. The following two verses refer more clearly to an embodied soul or psychic being.

> Katha II. 3. 17. "The purusha, the inner self, who is no larger than a thumb is seated always in the hearts of men. One must separate Him with patience from one's own body as one sepa-

> rates from a blade of grass its main fibre. Thou should know Him as the pure, the immortal, yea, as the pure, the immortal."

A similar verse is found in Shvetashvatara Upanishad, Verse III. 13:

> "The purusha, the inner self, who is no larger than a thumb is seated always in the hearts of men. He is the lord of the knowledge framed by the heart and the mind. They who know that become immortal."

For ordinary people psychic being remains veiled under the outer consciousness and is not developed enough to influence the outer nature or personality. In such cases one of the other purushas — mental, vital, or physical — takes the lead in controlling and/or influencing the outer nature. For many persons who have developed strong intellect it is the mind that becomes the leader. In such cases the mental purusha is commonly mistaken as the central being or soul. The mental Purusha is experienced as witness consciousness. Eventually, however, as further progress is made in the process of spiritual evolution, the psychic being becomes more developed and it begins to emerge in front and influence the outer personality. The emergence of psychic being is an important step forward in Sri Aurobindo's yoga.

## Concluding Remarks

For Hindu spiritual practice self-realization is of utmost importance. Self may be realized and experienced in different ways depending on the spiritual path followed by a spiritual seeker, and a sound knowledge of the various statuses of Self helps a seeker understand his own experiences. However, the concepts related to Self can be difficult to understand and confusing because of different views held by various philosophers on this subject and also for different terms used to define various modes or statuses of Self. Sri Aurobindo has been very precise and consistent in his writings with regard to the definitions of various terms. In most cases his concepts and definitions are compatible with those of traditional Hinduism, but in a few cases he presents unique concepts based on his personal experience.

Sri Aurobindo's philosophy places great importance on the role of an individual in the evolution of consciousness, and in this context the concept of psychic being is a valuable contribution to philosophy and spiritual practice. The emergence of psychic being is an essential step of the yogic path laid out by Sri Aurobindo, and usually it is followed by the realization of jivatman and Atman. The experience of jivatman leads to the attainment of cosmic consciousness, which reveals the unity of all beings in the universe.

It must be kept in mind that the different statuses of Self are not completely separate from each other; they are unified intimately and exist simultaneously. Sri Aurobindo points out repeatedly that an individual being in the world is a becoming of Supreme Self (Paramatman), and the world too is a becoming of the Supreme Self. In his own words the true self of an individual person (Jiva) "is a universal being in its relations with others and with Nature and in its upward term a portion or the living front of a supreme transcendent Spirit." (SY, p. 282) When an individual person gets rid of his ego he can embrace and include the universe in his consciousness; however, in doing so he does not abolish his spiritual individuality. Moreover, an individual's self, or soul, is connected with Supreme Self (Paramatman) not only because it is made of the same divine substance, but also because the Supreme Self, in its personal form of Ishwara, is present in the spiritual heart of an individual although he may not be aware of His presence due to ignorance. Gita repeatedly points out that "the Lord (Ishwara) is seated in the heart of all beings". (Verse XVIII — 61)

**Acknowledgement**

This article is a revised version of an article titled "Reality and Self According to Vedanta as Explained by Sri Aurobindo", which was published in *Mother India*, January 2016.

**References**

Radhakrishnan, S., *The Principal Upanishads*, Harper Collins Publishers India Private Ltd, 1994

Sri Aurobindo, *The Life Divine*, Sri Aurobindo Ashram Trust, Pondicherry, India, 8th Indian Printing, June 1973 [In the article this book is referenced as LD]

Sri Aurobindo, *Essays on the Gita*, Sri Aurobindo Ashram Trust, Pondicherry, India, 1976 [In the article this book is referenced as EG]

Sri Aurobindo, *The Synthesis of Yoga*, Sri Aurobindo Ashram Trust, Pondicherry, India, Sixth Edition, 1976 [In the article this book is referenced as SY]

Sri Aurobindo, *Letters on Yoga*, Part 1, Sri Aurobindo Ashram Trust, Pondicherry, India, Fourth Edition, 1971 [In the article this book is referenced as LY]

## Chapter 3

# God and World According to Spinoza and Vedanta

### Introduction

Most common persons in all societies — western and eastern — believe in God; however, their concepts, or ideas, of God and His relation with the world are not exactly alike. [I will use the word 'world' in the sense of phenomenal world, which includes the entire universe of which both the earth and its inhabitants are a part. This is the world insofar as it is perceptible and scientifically comprehensible to us as human beings.] Many persons accept the views of scriptures, which describe the glory of God, while philosophers debate on the existence of God and His characteristics. This article will not deal with the proofs for and against the existence of God, and it will begin with the premise that God exists and present the views about God as held by a few different theologies and philosophies of different cultures. The focus of the article will be on the views of Baruch Spinoza (1632 — 1677) on God's characteristics, or attributes, and His relation with the phenomenal world. One question to be examined is whether God is immaterial or whether He has both immaterial and material attributes. Other issues to be examined are God's transcendence and immanence with respect to the world and whether He is personal or impersonal. I should point out that Spinoza's philosophy covers a wide range of topics and issues such as freedom and causality, knowledge, emotions, virtue and happiness, and others. This article's scope will be limited to only the nature of God and His relation with the world.

In addition to Spinoza's own views I will present the prevailing theological and philosophical views of the West during his time to provide a background since his views were very different from his predecessors. I will also present a brief comparison of Spinoza's views with those of Vedanta philosophy of India, which is the most prominent school of Hindu philosophy. Views of Vedanta will be presented immediately following Spinoza's views on each question and issue that will be examined.

## Western Theology and Philosophy in Spinoza's Time

For western theology I will review the traditional Judeo-Christian views of God and the world, and for western philosophy I will present very briefly the views of the famous philosophers Aristotle (384 BC — 322 BC) and Rene Descartes (1596 — 1650 CE) who influenced Spinoza's thinking. My review will be brief.

The views of Judaism and Christianity on God and the world are dualistic. The dualism shows up at two levels. At one level dualism deals with the relation of God with the world, and at another level it deals with the relation of mind, or soul, with body. With regard to God's relation with the world Judaism and Christianity believe that God is the creator of the world and stands apart from it although he is not aloof. This view is found in Islam also. In Judaism and Christianity there are two views regarding the process of creation of the world. According to one view God created the world out of pre-existing matter and the other view is that He created the world out of nothing (*creatio ex nihilo*). In either case there is an absolute distinction between God and His creation. In addition it is generally believed that God is immaterial whereas the created world is material. With regard to dualism at the level of the world and its inhabitants it is widely believed in the west that all the objects of the world including the body of human beings are made of matter, but the soul is immaterial and separable from the body. (Soul in this context includes at least some aspects of mind and frequently a body's life-force also.) According to Genesis 2 of Old Testament God breathes life into the body of a person at the time of birth, and this view is expressed in Verses 2 - 7: "And the Lord God formed man of the dust of the ground, and breathed into his nostrils the breath of life; and man became a living being." Both Judaism and Christianity accept this view even if not always in completely literal terms. Thus at the world level the body and soul of human beings are, or are made of, two different substances. It is also not generally believed that the substance of human soul is, or is part of, the divine substance of God, if God can be said to have a substance. Thus man can come close to God but can never unite or merge with Him. In metaphysical terms the traditional view of Judaism and Christianity does not accept the immanence of God in the world, and instead it emphasizes the transcendence of God. It should be acknowledged that there are a few exceptions within these religions since some of the mystical schools of these religions such as Kabbalah of Judaism and Sufism of Islam do not accept the absolute separation and difference between God and man.

Another important aspect of Judaic-Christian and Islamic view of God is that God is a person. This concept is clearly implied in both Old and New Testaments and also Koran. Common persons of Jewish, Christian and Islamic faiths view God as an omniscient and omnipotent person, and they believe that there is a reciprocal relation between God and human beings. A personal God is not aloof from His creation, and He responds to human prayers. A personal God also expects human beings to love Him and obey His dictates.

I mentioned earlier that the famous philosophers Aristotle (384—322 B.C.E.) and Rene Descartes (1596 — 1650 CE) influenced Spinoza's thinking. Moses Maimonides (1135 — 1204 CE), a Jewish philosopher, also had considerable influence on Spinoza. However, Spinoza did not agree with their views completely. Aristotle did not accept the dualism of Plato, which separates abstract 'forms' of individual things of the world from the concrete things themselves. For Aristotle matter and form of individual things are inseparable and form is immanent in matter as the essence of a thing made out of that matter. It seems that Aristotle made an exception with regard to the form of intellectual activity, which is immanent within a living human being engaged in such activity and also seems to have an eternal existence apart from the matter of that being.

According to Aristotle both matter and form were preexisting and when the world came into being these two came together to form the composite substance of living things of the world. For Aristotle God is separate from the world. God is pure actuality and immaterial, and He is different from the substance of things of the world although he is its final cause. Aristotle referred to God as the 'unmoved mover' of the motion, i.e., causal changes, of the world. God set the world in motion and caused the potentiality hidden in the substance of the world to become actuality. Another noteworthy feature of Aristotle's concept of God is that He does not have personality, and this concept is contrary to the views of Judaism, Christianity, and Islam, which portray God as a person who is to be loved and worshipped.

Descartes is considered by many as the father of modern philosophy. He believed that God is immutable and immaterial, and that He created a mutable world of matter and minds. It is frequently said that according to Descartes bodies and minds are made of two different substances — bodies are made of corporeal substance, or matter, and minds are made of incorporeal substance. However, it is more accurate to say that minds *are* incorporeal "substances" for Descartes. They are substances in the sense that they can only possibly exist if God creates them individually, and they can only cease to exist if God no longer continues them in existence. The matter of which bodies are composed and all individual minds are created substances, and this metaphysical view is a form of what is known as substance dualism. However, it is difficult to understand how Descartes thinks about minds, if he does not think of them as made out of any substance. According to some scholars, Descartes thinks of minds as composed of nothing but mental activity or thinking. In any case he says that mental activity or thinking is their "essence." Further, it is not clear whether God can be said to be made of any substance for Descartes. However, if He is, then that substance is different from any other substance. Descartes describes the essence or principal attribute of God as "infinite perfection," which includes omniscience and omnipotence.

## Spinoza's Philosophy of God and Vedanta's

Spinoza was a Jew of Spanish descent, and he lived in Amsterdam in Netherlands. He presented a very different view of God from the traditional western theology and philosophy. His view was considered so radically different from the prevalent view of Judaism about God that he was excommunicated from the Jewish community of Amsterdam. In this section I will review the major elements of Spinoza's view related to God and point out those elements or concepts that are very different from those of his time. I also will compare Spinoza's view with that of Vedanta. In a latter section I will discuss his view on God's relation with the world.

Metaphysical Monism

The widely accepted view prevailing at the time of Spinoza was that the world, which is created by God, is made of two different substances — matter and mind, and that these substances are different from the immaterial substance of God. Spinoza did not accept this dualistic view of different substances. He believed that there is only one substance, which is God. In Part 1 of his famous book, *Ethics*, he presented in a systematic way the definitions and propositions of terms and concepts related to God and the world. (Shirley, 1982) I will present only a few selected definitions and propositions from the *Ethics* and also provide some explanation. I will compare some of these concepts with those of Vedanta.

Spinoza defined God as follows:

Definition 1 - 6: By God I mean an absolutely infinite Being; that is, substance consisting of infinite attributes, each of which expresses eternal and infinite essence.

Definition 1 - 3: By substance I mean that which is in itself and is conceived through itself; that is, that the conception of which does not require the conception of another thing from which it has to be formed.

Following these definitions of God and substance Spinoza presented many 'propositions', and the following three pertain to God and the world.

Proposition 1 - 7: Existence belongs to the nature of substance.

Proposition 1 - 14: There can be, or be conceived, no other substance but God.

Proposition 1 - 15: Whatever is, is in God, and nothing can be or be conceived without God.

It can be concluded from the above definitions and propositions that Spinoza believed in metaphysical monism according to which Reality is composed of only one substance, which was called God by Spinoza. He also believed that God is self-caused (*causa sui*) and independent whereas everything else is dependent on God. This monistic view is in sharp contrast with the Judaic-Christian theology's dualistic concept of God and the world. It also is different from the views of most western philosophers who believed in two, or more, substances. Further, Spinoza disagreed with western theology and philosophy of his time as to the characteristics of God. I will discuss a few of these characteristics, which are the materiality of God, the impersonal character of God, and natural laws.

## Vedanta's View on Monism

Spinoza's monism is compatible with the view of Vedanta. There is a famous verse in Chandogya Upanishad (Verse 3. 14.3), which says that "Verily, this whole world is Brahman." The Ultimate Reality in Vedanta philosophy is Brahman, and in its highest status Brahman is indeterminable. However, with reference to the manifested world it takes the poise of Atman, or Self, which becomes the inner essence, or substance, of everything that exists. Spinoza's Substance is very similar to Vedanta's Atman.

## Materiality of God

Traditional theology and philosophy of the west consider God as purely immaterial and treats the world as material. They consider God to be the efficient cause of the universe and they also proclaim God's omnipresence in the world, but they deny that God has any material aspects or attributes. This view naturally raises the question "How can an immaterial God create a material world?" A few theologians and philosophers who preceded Spinoza believed that matter was pre-existent. Christianity believes that matter was created out of nothing (*ex nihilo*). Both these views can be questioned. Even if we accept that matter was pre-existent, can we not still ask how an immaterial God could form a universe, or a world, out of that matter? The claim that matter was "created out of nothing" also is very difficult for many to accept since it goes against all principles of science. Spinoza could not accept either of these views.

Spinoza's view about the God's materiality is daringly different from prevailing views of his time. He declared in Proposition 1 - 14 of *The Ethics* that "There can be, or be conceived, no other substance but God". He also believed that the world is an emanation of God, or an emanation of the essence of God; so the materiality of the world must come from God's own substance. Spinoza also said in Proposition 1 - 11, "God or substance consisting of infinite attributes, each of which expresses eternal and infinite essence, necessarily exists", and according to him two of these attributes can be known by human intellect. These two knowable attributes of Substance are 'extension' and 'thought'. Spinoza's term 'extension' represents 'matter', and his 'thought' represents 'mind'. Spinoza's view that extension and thought are attributes of God, or substance, leads to the conclusion that everything within the universe including God has both material and immaterial aspects.

Vedanta's View on Materiality

Vedanta philosophy agrees with Spinoza on the question of materiality of God as it recognizes that the matter comes from the Ultimate Reality, Brahman. Taittiriya Upanishad (Verse 3. 2. 1) says, "He knew that matter is Brahman". This is meant to say that matter is an attribute of Brahman. According to Vedanta mind, or consciousness, also is an attribute, or power, of Brahman. In the process of self-manifestation matter emerges from Brahman.

## Personality of God and Love of God

Traditional religions emphasize the personal aspect of God. For them God has emotions and human beings can have a reciprocal relation with Him. God expects human beings to love Him and follow His dictates, and in return He also loves them. Traditional religions also believe that God rewards and punishes human beings after they die according to their actions in life. In contrast to these traditional views Spinoza believed that God is an impersonal entity with no emotions and also that God does not love or hate anyone. These views are presented in Proposition 5 - 17, which says, "God is without passive emotions, and he is not affected with any emotion of pleasure and pain". The Corollary of this Proposition says, "Strictly speaking God does not love or hate anyone".

It is interesting that despite his proclaiming God's impersonality Spinoza wrote about a man's 'intellectual love of God', which is a famous expression of Spinoza's philosophy. Spinoza discussed at length various levels or grades of knowledge. At the lowest level is the knowledge based on sense-perception, which yields superfluous knowledge of particular things. At the highest level is the knowledge that perceives the essence of particular things and develops a clear understanding about them. This knowledge helps us understand that particular things are in God and conceived through God. The clear understanding of particular things leads to an understanding of God and the idea of God as cause. (Propositions 5 - 24, and 5 - 32). According to Spinoza this type of understanding is the highest level of knowledge and he called it the third kind of knowledge. In Proposition 5 - 27 he wrote: "From this third kind of knowledge there arises the highest possible content of mind". Then in the *Corollary* of Proposition 5 - 32 he wrote that "from the third kind of knowledge there necessarily arises the intellectual love of God". This love is directed to God and it consists not of joy or passion, but blessedness itself.

## Vedanta's View on God's Personality

The issue of God having personality or not was debated vigorously by some of the great scholars of the past, who interpreted the original sources of Vedanta philosophy differently. Based on the differences in their views three different major schools of Vedanta were formed, and each had considerable following. For Adwaita (non-dual) Vedanta of Shankara the ultimate Reality is Brahman, which is impersonal without any personal qualities (*Nirguna*). The impersonality of Brahman is considered by this school as the supreme truth. However, Shankara recognized that as long as a human being lives in ignorance he would believe in a personal God with qualities (*Saguna*). The other two major schools of Vedanta did not accept Shankara's view that God can be impersonal. Both these schools recognized that the highest Reality is God with personality, Ishwara, and emphasized devotional spiritual practices, which are very popular among Hindus. In Gita the Supreme Person has been described in Verse 13 — 15 (or 13 —14 in some versions of Gita) as free from qualities yet enjoyer of qualities (*nirgunam gunabhoktr ca*). The concept of impersonal Brahman dominated early Upanishads, but references to a personal God can be found in later Upanishads such as Svetashvatara Upanishad. In Gita God (as Krishna) is a person and a friend of Arjuna and all human beings, and He encourages men in distress to come to Him for shelter and protection. This personal aspect of God is lacking is Spinoza's philosophy. As I mentioned earlier Spinoza wrote about 'intellectual love', which a person of a high level of knowledge has toward God. However, there is no suggestion in Spinoza's philosophy that God loves anybody.

Vedanta agrees with Spinoza's view that right kind of knowledge leads to love of God. Gita addressed this issue in depth. The spiritual practices discussed in Gita include three paths for finding God. These are the path of Knowledge, the path of Works, and the path of Devotion, which includes love and adoration. The path of knowledge involves the understanding of the oneness in the world and also understanding that the essence of everything is Brahman, the Ultimate Reality. According to Gita knowledge leads to love and also that knowledge combined with love and adoration of God is the best approach. The following verse is one of several verses in Gita that present this view:

Verse 7 — 17: Of those the person with knowledge, who is ever in constant union with the Divine, whose devotion is all concentrated on Him, is the best. The person of knowledge is dear to me, and I am dear to him.

## Relation of God with the World: Immanence and Transcendence

In the beginning of this section I will examine Spinoza's views related to the manifestation or emanation of the world. Then I will address the issue of God's immanence and transcendence with regard to the world.

Manifestation (or Emanation) of the World, Its Purpose, and Free Will

The common view of Western theologians and philosophers of Spinoza's time and earlier was that God created the world out of nothing or from preexisting matter, and in either case world's substance is non-divine, i.e., different from God. As I mentioned earlier, Spinoza could not accept this view. He repeatedly wrote that there cannot be more than one substance. He wrote in Proposition 1 - 25: "God is the efficient cause not only of the existence of things but also of their essence". In Proposition 1 - 15 Spinoza wrote: "God is the immanent, not transitive, cause of all things". These two propositions indicate that God is the efficient cause and also the inner essence, or inner being, of the world. That means that the world and everything in it in some way expresses God's being. The world is not a creation but an emanation of God.

A pertinent question related to God and the world is: is there any purpose for the existence of the world? Another question is: could the world have existed in another way? Spinoza believed that there is no hidden plan or goal for the existence of the world. He also believed that God does not have free will. Spinoza wrote in Proposition 1 - 29: "Nothing in nature is contingent, but all things are from the necessity of the divine nature determined to exist and to act in a definite way." In Proposition 1 - 33 he wrote: "Things could not have been produced by God in any other way or in any other order than is the case." Thus God acts by the necessity of His own nature and is incapable of changing the course of His actions, and this means that whatever exists is how it must be. The view of Spinoza that God acts by necessity of His own nature and does not have free will is very different from the views of traditional religions.

Another interesting concept of Spinoza's philosophy is related to free will and determinism with regard to the operation of the world and its inhabitants. According to Spinoza all events in the world are components of a causal chain in which everything happens necessarily as it does. From this it follows that human beings do not have any free will; their acts in the world are causally related and determined by God's nature, but not by any kind of divine will.

Vedanta's Views on Manifestation

The concept of manifestation of the phenomenal world as opposed to creation is fundamental for Vedanta philosophy, and so Vedanta is in agreement with Spinoza on this issue. The following verse of Mundaka Upanishad uses the example of a spider and how it spins its thread and makes a web to illustrate how God manifested the phenomenal world out of itself.

Mundaka 1. 1. 7: As a spider creates and withdraws (its thread/web), as herbs grow on earth, as the hair (grows) on the head and the body of a living person, so from the Imperishable arises here the universe.

However, apart from any question as to how literally we should take such metaphors, there is a difference between Spinoza's views and those of Vedanta as to the purpose of manifestation. For Spinoza God manifested the world from the necessity of his own Nature. Vedanta does not agree with this view. There are different views within Vedanta as to why the Ultimate Reality, Brahman, manifested the world. The Vedanta philosophy of Shankara does not accept the world as truly real, but it fails to explain why the world came into being even at an illusory level if the goal of human life should be to get out of it and merge with Brahman. The schools of Vedanta belonging to Ramanuja and Madhva believe that the manifestation is real and it is for the sport or play (*Lila*) of God. Contemporary scholars of Vedanta such as Swami Vivekananda and Sri Aurobindo believe in teleology of the manifestation. They believe in spiritual evolution, i.e., evolution of consciousness, which would lead to the development of higher levels on consciousness in human beings and the establishment of more harmonious communities.

With reference to Spinoza's view on free will and determinism, which I discussed earlier very briefly, I should point out that Vedanta philosophy admits determinism in the form of the doctrine of *Karma* according to which a person's actions are components of a chain of causes and effects. This view is compatible with that of Spinoza. However, Vedanta also admits the freedom of choice, or free will. Vedanta believes that although most events and the actions of persons occur *necessarily*, a person can have free will if he is highly conscious and aware of his choices and their consequences. I have discussed this issue of free will and determinism in depth in another chapter of this book, which is titled "Free will and determinism according to Vedanta and western philosophy".

God's Immanence and Transcendence

A common interpretation of Spinoza's philosophy is that his God is identical to Nature, i.e., in the sense of the phenomenal world, and nothing more; this concept is commonly known as pantheism. However, even though this view allows that the phenomenal world may have aspects or dimensions not evident to either ordinary perception or even to the understanding of natural science, some scholars believe that this interpretation is still not correct, and I will present their arguments.

Spinoza followed medieval thinkers in distinguishing between *Natura Naturans* and *Natura Naturata*, and to understand Spinoza's metaphysics it is necessary to know clearly how he understood and used these two expressions. The first expression, *Natura Naturans*, literally means 'nature naturing', or nature qua actively expressing; it is the inner essence of whatever is or happens. In the Scholium of Proposition 1 - 29 Spinoza referred to it as "God in so far as he is considered a free cause". This means that God, or *Natura Naturans*, is not determined by anything but itself. It is a creative or productive principle that is eternally producing what Spinoza calls infinitely many "modes", or "modifications", and also sustains them. *Natura Naturata* literally means 'nature natured', and in Spinoza's own words it is "all that follows from the necessity of God's nature" (Scholium of Proposition 1 — 29). It thus refers to the manifested Nature, which includes all modes. *Natura Naturata* is thus seemingly not identical to *Natura Naturans*, and Spinoza describes it, or at least everything within it, as something that can only be conceived as *in* God. Even though they are seemingly not identical Spinoza frequently writes as if his God in some sense "is" both *Natura Naturans* and *Natura Naturata.* Insofar as God is more than *Natura Naturata,* it can be argued that God in some sense transcends the world. In this sense, in Wolfson's words, "Spinoza's substance is thus a whole transcending the universe, the latter being the sum of the modes". (p. Vol. II, 74, 75) At the same time, since it is expressing, or "naturing," itself in all modes as the inner essence, God as substance is also immanent in the world.

It should be emphasized that Spinoza's God is not transcendent in the sense that he is separate from the modes, even if in some way distinct from them. He is not a creator who stands apart from his creation. He is transcendent and immanent with respect to the phenomenal world simultaneously. There is an ontological unity between God and the world of modes.

There are two other reasons for making the case that Spinoza's God has a transcendent aspect. First, Spinoza argued that there must be an infinite number of attributes of God, even if only two of those — thought and extension — are expressed in the Nature, which is the world insofar as it is perceptible and scientifically comprehensible to us as human beings. (Nature is composed of all the Modes). So since God has more attributes (than the Nature), it is more than the Nature. Second, Spinoza treated God and its attributes as being eternal. This has two implications — (i) God, or Substance, is outside time or duration, and (ii) God is immutable. In contrast to this status of God the world of Modes, i.e., *Natura Naturata,* is in time and is mutable. In a letter to Ludwig Meyer, Spinoza wrote: "It is to the existence of Modes only that we can apply the term Duration; the corresponding term for the existence of Substance is Eternity, ...". (Shirley, p. 232). I would like to point out that the question whether God is also outside space is difficult to answer. In any case it appears that the metaphysical structure of Spinoza's philosophy should be treated as panentheism, not pantheism.

## Vedanta's View on Immanence and Transcendence

Vedanta agrees with Spinoza's views regarding the transcendence and immanence of God with respect to the world. The ultimate Reality, Brahman, which also is Self (Atman), transcends the world in two senses. Self represents the thing-in-itself of the phenomenal world, and it also is outside space and time. Simultaneous with being transcendent Self is immanent in the world since it is the essence of everything. In Gita Sri Krishna makes this concept very clear to Arjuna. In Verse 9 — 4, He says, "By Me all this universe is pervaded through my unmanifested form. All beings abide in Me but I do not abide in them". The meaning of this verse is that God is immanent in the world and everything in the world is contained in Him, but He is much more than the world and the world cannot contain Him fully. The immanence of God is expressed in many verses of the Upanishads and the Gita. Verse 2 — 17 of Svetasvatara Upanishad says, "The God who is in fire, who is in water, who has entered into the whole world, who is in plants, who is in trees, to that God be adoration, yea, be adoration". There is another similarity between Spinoza's views and those of Vedanta. In Vedanta there is a creative principle of God, which manifests the world, and it is referred to as the Supreme Nature, or *Para Prakiti*. This principle is similar to *Natura Naturans* of Spinoza.

It should be pointed out that there may be a difference between Spinoza and Vedanta as to the definition of transcendence. Spinoza's God is the thing-in-itself of all modes, which constitutes the phenomenal world, and this is similar to Vedanta's Self. As I discussed earlier for Spinoza God is outside time duration, but he was not clear on the question whether God is outside space also. For Vedanta God (or Brahman) clearly is outside both space and time and also immanent in the world. Brahman is even beyond Self or Atman.

## Summary and Closing Comments

Spinoza is one of the greatest philosophers of all times. He was knowledgeable of the philosophical and theological views of his time, but he had an independent mind and he developed his own views, which were radically different from the prevailing views. His views were so different that he was excommunicated from the Jewish community of Amsterdam where he lived. I have presented in this article his views related to God and His relation with the world. I will review his views again very briefly.

Spinoza's philosophy is dominated by the principle of unity and it represents monism. He declared that the world is a manifestation of God, who is substance, and that both mind and matter are attributes of the substance. He rejected the traditional view that God is purely immaterial and He stands apart from His creation, which is material. God of traditional religions expects human beings to follow His dictates. Spinoza's God is impersonal, devoid of emotions, and He is immaterial as well as material. Spinoza's God is immanent in the world, but He is more than the world and can be considered to be transcendent also.

Vedanta philosophy agrees with Spinoza's views on certain issues, but it has differences too. Vedanta too represents monism and its philosophy unifies God and the manifested world. However, there is a strong theistic aspect of Vedanta, which is missing in Spinoza's philosophy. Although Spinoza discussed the concept of 'intellectual love of God', which is the love of human beings directed to God, his God is impersonal and has no emotions. According to Vedanta God has an impersonal aspect as well as a personal aspect. Human beings can love God and God also loves human beings. The personal aspect of God plays a very important role in the spiritual practices related to Vedanta.

Before closing I want to point out that this article is of limited scope. Spinoza's philosophy covers a variety of subjects and many of those were not examined in this article.

## Brief Bibliography

Hampshire, Stuart, *Spinoza*, Penguin Books, 1951

Shirley, Samuel, *Baruch Spinoza: The Ethics and Selected Letters*, Hackett Publishing Company, 1982

Scruton, Roger, *Spinoza: A very Short Introduction*, Oxford University Press, 2002

Wolfson, Harry, A., "Spinoza and the Religion of the Past", *Religious Philosophy: A Group of Essays*, Atheneum, NY, 1961

Wolfson, Harry, A., *The Philosophy of Spinoza, Volume I*, Schocken Books, 1969

Wolfson, Harry, A., *The Philosophy of Spinoza, Volume II*, Schocken Books, 1969

# Chapter 4

# Schopenhauer and Indian Philosophies

## Introduction

Interest of western scholars in Indian philosophies grew primarily in the twentieth century. During the nineteenth century there were very few western scholars who had any knowledge of Indian philosophies, and one of the reasons was that books on Indian philosophies and/or translations of Indian religious texts in European languages were not easily available. So it is quite remarkable that a philosopher of the stature of Arthur Schopenhauer (1788 — 1860) took keen interest in reading translations of Upanishads, Bhagavad Gita (or simply Gita) and also Samkhya Karika of *Ishwara* Krishna. He also had read translations of a few Buddhist texts.

Schopenhauer belongs to a golden period of German philosophy filled with famous philosophers. Among those who preceded him is Immanuel Kant (1724 — 1804), whose philosophy he studied thoroughly. Johann G. Fichte (1762 — 1814) and Friedrich W. J. Schelling (1775 —1854) were just a little ahead of him, and Schopenhauer actually attended few courses given by Fichte. In addition to Fichte and Schelling, Georg W. F. Hegel (1770 — 1831) was his contemporary. Actually the fame and prominence of Hegel in the world of philosophy at that time overshadowed Schopenhauer and his work until very late in his life. Schopenhauer did not like Hegel's philosophy and he did not hide his bitter feelings about him. He also did not like the philosopies of Fichte and Schelling, although scholars have pointed out certain affinities between Schopenhauer and Schelling. Among those who came a little later Karl Marx (1818 — 1883) and Friedrich Nietzsche (1844 — 1900) are well known. There is no indication that any of these great philosophers except Schopenhauer and to some extent Nietzsche had any significant exposure to Indian philosophy.

Schopenhauer was the first among the great western philosophers who recognized the value of Indian philosophies and made numerous references to Indian philosophical concepts in his own writings. It is reported that late in life he read Upanishads every night. In one of his publications in his late years, referring to Upanishads, he wrote:

> It is the most profitable and sublime reading that is possible in the world; it has been the consolation of my life and will be that of my death. (Schopenhauer 1851, p. 397)

Schopenhauer's philosophy was known to many Indian scholars and spiritual leaders of the twentieth century. On more than one occasion in his lectures Swami Vivekananda made reference to Schopenhauer and his admiration of Indian philosophies. In a lecture delivered in Colombo, Sri Lanka, Swami Vivekananda referred to Schopenhauer as the "great German sage" although he did not agree with all aspects of Schopenhauer's philosophy. (Swami Vivekananda, 1947, p. 109) Sri Aurobindo too regarded Schopenhauer as a 'great intellect' and having a 'mind of the greatest power' in the field of philosophy, and he appreciated the fact that Schopenhauer recognized the greatness of Indian philosophies. (Sri Aurobindo, 1968, p. 16 and 48)

A few questions that have been raised about Schopenhauer's encounter with and knowledge of Indian philosophies include the following: (1) What influence did Schopenhauer's initial contact with Indian philosophies have on his own philosophy as it began to develop; and (2) Did Indian philosophies influence Schopenhauer strongly enough so that he actually changed some of his early views in his later writings. These issues are difficult to resolve. The scholars who examined these issues include Urs App (2006), Moira Nicholls (Nicholls 1999) and Douglas L. Berger (Berger 2004). I will not deal with these issues in this article; instead I will address a more straightforward question: what are the similarities and differences between Schopenhauer's philosophy and Indian philosophies?

This article is organized in two parts. In the first part I will present a brief overview of Schopenhauer's own philosophy and I will discuss certain key metaphysical concepts and also his views on the meaning of life and the way for salvation. In the second part I will discuss how he became acquainted with Indian philosophies, and I will make a comparison of his philosophy with Indian philosophies. Among Indian philosophies I will focus primarily on Vedanta philosophy, which is based on interpretations of Upanishads, and Samkhya Karika as well as Buddhism since he was familiar with these three schools of thought. I should point out that Hinduism includes both Vedanta and Samkhya Karika.

The reference sources for Schopenhauer's philosophy will be primarily the two volumes of his most famous work, which are titled: *The World as Will and Presentation, Volume One*, which was originally published in 1819, and *The World as Will and Presentation, Volume Two*, which was originally published in 1844. Both volumes were written in German. The English translations of these books, which I will use, are: Volume One by Richard E. Aquila in 2008, and Volume Two by David Carus and Richard E. Aquila in 2010. (I may point out that the translation of volume one is based on the third edition of the book published in 1859.)

## Part I
## Schopenhauer's Philosophy

### Metaphysical Aspects

Most of Schopenhauer's philosophy is coherent and straightforward. However, there are a few aspects of his philosophy dealing with metaphysical concepts that are seemingly incoherent and difficult, if not impossible, to explain. Schopenhauer himself seems to have been aware of the problem and had difficulty in reconciling the inconsistencies. I will point out some of these inconsistencies when we will encounter them in this discussion, but I will not be able to provide an in-depth explanation of these issues. I may add that some of the inconsistencies may have been brought about by his attempt to incorporate ideas from Indian philosophies, especially the Upanishads.

The basic structure of Schopenhauer's metaphysical thought is somewhat similar to that of Immanuel Kant's philosophy, which he studied thoroughly and also critiqued. According to Schopenhauer the world has two aspects — appearance and thing-in-itself. First, the world is an appearance or presentation of objects to individual cognizant subjects. The world as appearance is what Immanuel Kant called 'phenomenon'. The second aspect is the inner essence, or thing-in-itself, and with respect to this aspect of his philosophy he differed from Kant, who believed that the true nature of objects and subjects, i.e., things-in-themselves, cannot be known by us and that they belong to a different realm, which he called 'noumenon'. Kant believed that it could in principle only be known in a purely intellectual way. According to Schopenhauer the true inner essence, i.e., thing-in-itself, of everything in the phenomenal world is a force, which he called Will, and it is known to us by a particular sort of feeling of our own inner being. In the next section I will present more information about these two aspects.

## Appearance and Thing-in-Itself

When referring to the appearance aspect of the world Schopenhauer uses the German word 'Vorstellung', which has been translated by different translators as 'idea', 'representation', and also 'presentation'. In a recent translation of Schopenhauer's book *Die Welt als Wille und Vorstellung*, Richard Aquila carefully chose to translate the word Vorstellung as 'presentation', and he points out that the word Vorstellung is commonly used to refer to theatrical presentation (Aquila, 2008). Schopenhauer speaks of appearance as having two sides — object and subject, which are interdependent and inseparable although distinct from each other. So the world's appearance consists of objects that are presented to an individual subject's mental theater and the subject observes them in the way a spectator of a theatrical presentation does. The subject may also become emotionally involved with the appearance. Schopenhauer makes a distinction between individual subjects and 'the Subject'. I will discuss the concept of individual subjects first and I will explain the concept of the Subject a little later. At present I would like to point out briefly that for Schopenhauer an individual subject is a part of the phenomenon whereas 'the Subject' is universal, or cosmic, in nature and is outside phenomenon.

Objects include all physical items of the world including a subject's own body, and they are known by a subject by way of sensory perception. It is important to note that Schopenhauer believes in idealism, but his idealism is not of the extreme type that considers objects as purely mental constructions. He tried to draw a balance between materialism and idealism although he believed strongly in many aspects of idealism. He called himself a transcendental idealist similar to Immanuel Kant. (According to transcendental idealism the world may legitimately be regarded as 'appearances' of things that are fundamentally real, i.e., things are not merely mental constructions but exist in space and time.) Schopenhauer regarded individual subjects themselves as objects existing in space and time.

Objects coexist with individual subjects. Schopenhauer called individual subjects as willing subjects or subjects of will. It is central to Schopenhauer's philosophy that objects and individual subjects are not derived from two different principles; their inner essence is the same principle — the thing-in-itself. (I am referring to individual subjects in this context and not 'the Subject'.) The thing-in-itself, or inner essence, is what he called Will, and it is the single principle that constitutes everything in the world ranging from dense matter like a rock to apparently immaterial things such as desires, emotions and even the functioning of intelligence. According to Schopenhauer anything physical in nature is an objectification of Will, and he went into great details to explain how Will is objectified at various levels of objects. Schopenhauer viewed this objectification as occurring on increasingly developed levels of gradation, the most developed gradation being that of the human being. He also pointed out the increasingly developed quality of cognizance associated with the various grades of objectification of Will. For example, whereas animals rely on perception and instincts humans have an additional faculty of intellect. The quality of cognizance is highest at the human level. Schopenhauer associated the levels of gradation with something comparable to distinct Platonic Ideas or Forms. However, he also believed that all objects — from the most obviously material to the seemingly immaterial — are subject to natural causal laws. This is dictated by a particular form of the Principle of Sufficient Reason to which everything that is an object of *Vorstellung* is subject. The Principle of Sufficient Reason was expounded also by other philosophers, perhaps most notably by Gottfried Leibniz (1646 — 1716). Schopenhauer, however, developed a more detailed explanation of this principle, distinguishing four varieties of it according to four different kinds of 'object' of *Vorstellung*: sensory appearances, physical events, abstract concepts, and the willing subject, which is a special kind of 'object.' He first presented this in his 1813 doctoral dissertation *On the Fourfold Root of the Principle of Sufficient Reason* (Second Edition, 1847).

Schopenhauer's Will is 'blind striving' and it has no purpose or aim to fulfill; it is basically a force that is felt as an urge and expressed in all activities of nature including actions for survival, procreation and even intellectual thinking. Since in the ordinary sense the word 'will' implies a strong determination to fulfill a purpose or goal and since Schopenhauer's Will does not have any purpose, a question arises as to why Schopenhauer chose to use the word Will instead of 'force' or 'energy'. According to Schopenhauer he chose the word Will because it is only through a feeling of the expression our own 'will' that we can get some idea in the concrete sense of what sort of force he is referring to.

I pointed out earlier that with regard to the thing-in-itself of the phenomenon, Schopenhauer disagreed with Kant. According to Kant the things-in-themselves of objects of the phenomenal world cannot be known by us; but according to Schopenhauer the thing-in-itself can be known and he declared it to be the single principle of Will. For Schopenhauer the manifestations of Will in the phenomenal world operate in space and time and follow the laws of cause and effect, but Will itself, as the thing-in-itself, is outside space and time, just as is the one Subject.

## Subjects of Different Types

The concepts of a subject (or self), and cognizance (or consciousness) associated with it, are a little complicated in Schopenhauer's philosophy since he postulates a few different types of subjects or self in different contexts, and this topic deserves careful attention. As Janaway points out,

> In his philosophy the self is seen successively as a subject of experience and knowledge, a subject of will and action, a bodily manifestation of will to life, and a pure mirror of timeless reality. Sometimes it is as if a struggle for dominance is being waged between these different conceptions. (Janaway, 2002, p. 50)

There are some incoherencies in Schopenhauer's explanation of how these different types of subjects are related to Will and also with each other. It is not possible to resolve all inconsistencies, and I will present a few possible interpretations, and I acknowledge the possibility of other explanations.

First, I will discuss Schopenhauer's willing subject or 'subject of will'. Individual willing subjects are also cognizant subjects, and their inner essence is, like that of all objects, Will, which is manifesting itself in the phenomenal world. Therefore, they are all material entities. According to Schopenhauer this subject is an individual because of the principle of individuation (*principium individuationis*), which recognizes the *a priori* determining character of space and time. This subject is an individual also because of its special relation with a single body. An individual self is subject to egoism and associated pain and pleasure. In Schopenhauer's words an individual willing subject "makes himself the centre of the world, has regard for his own existence and well-being before any other". (Schopenhauer 1819, p. 388) This self is driven by desire, lust, and other tendencies that bring to it nothing but ultimate misery. This willing subject plays a key role in Schopenhauer's pessimistic philosophy of life.

Schopenhauer believes in a single cosmic Will manifesting itself in all individual willing subjects. But he never speaks of this Will as itself a willing Subject, i.e., a cosmic willing subject. He does sometime speak of it as 'becoming' a multiplicity of willing subjects. He may be taken to mean that a multiplicity of bodies, whose inner being is Will, become willing subjects by virtue of their cognizance by brain functions. Schopenhauer's concept of individual willing subjects is straight forward and free from controversies. However, it is interesting to note that although this individual self of will is what most persons identify with and it seems to be very real to an ordinary individual, in reality this egoist self is somewhat fictitious, and Schopenhauer explains this as follows:

> This *cognizant* and conscious I is related to the will that is the basis of its phenomenon as the image in the focus of the concave mirror to the latter itself and, like that image, has only a conditioned, indeed strictly speaking a merely seeming reality." (Schopenhauer 1844, p. 317)

I may point out that the concept of an individual willing subject is similar to that of an 'ego self' (Ahamkara) of Hinduism. I will discuss this later.

Now let us examine the Subject of knowledge. In addition to individual willing subjects Schopenhauer presents the concept of 'the Subject', which is a cosmic or universal Subject, and this also plays an important role in his philosophy. Schopenhauer himself did not use the terms cosmic or universal in this regard, but his description of the Subject is at least compatible with the concept of a cosmic Subject. In the beginning portions of Volume One of his book *The World as Will and Presentation* Schopenhauer describes the Subject as "that which is cognizant of all things and of which none is cognizant". (Schopenhauer 1819, p. 33) He also says a little later that the Subject "does not lie within space and time; for it is whole and undivided in every being that is engaged in presentation." (Schopenhauer 1819, p. 34) According to Schopenhauer the objects of the world are in space and time and are affected by the laws of cause and effect, but the Subject of knowledge is not any sort of object to be found in the world. The Subject is nonetheless in some way "present" undivided in every perceiving being, and thus it is, in some sense, a universal or cosmic Subject. One of his favorite statements with reference to the Subject of knowledge, which he repeats on several occasions, is that it is "the world's *one eye* that looks out from all cognizant beings." (Schopenhauer 1819, p. 242) Schopenhauer calls this Subject the pure Subject of cognition, free of any motivation derived from Will. The Subject is not matter and is not constituted by Will. It is pure consciousness and will-less. According to Schopenhauer this Subject develops the very world of presentation within which all things exist through modes of awareness/cognizance and perception that comprise the subject 'side' of appearance. As a heuristic fiction Schopenhauer envisioned that before individual objects and subjects are manifested in the phenomenal world there is a stage when Matter in an undifferentiated state and a universal Subject stand as the two poles of the world as presentation. (He discussed this concept in the first chapter of the second volume of his book *The World as Will and Presentation.*) Furthermore, it is only in some sort of union of this Matter with the Subject that there comes to be constituted, as objects for the Subject, a world of objects that can be thought of as made of matter. Now on the side of individual cognizant subjects, Schopenhauer seems to suggest that the single universal Subject is instantiated in all instances of cognition, and that the bodies of individual subjects provide the medium of the Subject's expression; in other words, it is by union with individual bodies that a single Subject of knowledge appears as multiple subjects of knowledge. However, the concept of multiple non-physical subjects of knowledge, which are derived from the Subject, comes into a conflict with that of individual willing subjects, which are physical entities.

One way to resolve this conflict of two types of individual subjects is to accept the Subject of Knowledge only as a cosmic or universal Subject. We may also recognize that this Subject of knowledge can be experienced by an individual in special cases, but ordinarily it is only the willing subject that is experienced. Actually Schopenhauer himself seems to suggest that an individual has two categories of cognizance. In most cases an individual is engrossed in egoistic natural cognizance, which is colored by motivations arising from will, and this is the ordinary cognizance commonly found in a willing subject or self. However, this cognizance is *capable of becoming* purified of motivation arising from will and then one can experience will-less awareness or cognizance of the cosmic Subject, which manifests undivided in individuals. Schopenhauer states that there are also certain exceptional cases, associated with either aesthetic contemplation or the complete denial of one's will on the part of an ascetic 'saint,' when will-less cognizance manifests in an individual. In these cases the Subject is "present" undivided in every instance of will-less cognition. One of Schopenhauer's favorite statements with reference to the Subject of knowledge, which he repeats on several occasions, is that it is "the world's *one eye* that looks out from all cognizant beings." (Schopenhauer 1819, p. 242).

Schopenhauer's distinction between the two types of subjects, one being the individual self of willing and cognizance, and the other the pure Subject of cognition or the eternal world eye, is amplified in the following statement of his, which he included in Volume Two:

> ... we can attribute a twofold existence to every person. As will, and therefore as individual, he is only one and this one exclusively, which leaves him fully occupied with doing and suffering. As that which is engaged in purely objective presentation, he is the pure subject of cognizance, in whose consciousness alone the objective world has its existence. As such he is *all things*, insofar as he perceives them, and in him their existence is apart from burden and hardship. It is, namely, *his* existence, insofar as it exists in *his* presentation; but it is there apart from will. By contrast, insofar as it is will, it is not in him. All is well with one in the state in which he is all things; all is woe where he is exclusively a single one. (Schopenhauer 1844, p. 421)

There is one issue with the above described interpretation of the nature of two types of subject which should be noted. This interpretation introduces two different principles operating in the world — one is Will and the other is the Subject, and this makes Schopenhauer a dualist. An alternative interpretation is to treat the Subject in its inner being as the same thing as Will. According to this other view it is Will that becomes conscious at certain levels of its manifestation, beginning with animal life and in the most elevated form in human life and consciousness. Indeed there are some statements of Schopenhauer that actually support this view. I discussed this earlier. This view makes Schopenhauer a materialist, which may not be a problem since he himself acknowledged the strong materialistic orientation of his philosophy. However, there is a problem with this purely materialistic view since it would make it impossible for the purification of consciousness and the denial of Will to occur. The denial of Will is a major part of Schopenhauer's philosophy, which I will discuss in a following section.

### Critique of Schopenhauer's Metaphysical Structure

For the most part Schopenhauer's philosophy has a coherent theme, which is that everything in the world is material, and further that the essence of everything in the world is Will, which is blind striving. According to him even dense matter is an objectification of Will. Furthermore, this force (i.e., Will) is 'One' although it appears as many objects. This materialistic theme is fairly straightforward although some may disagree with its basic tenet. However, this metaphysical scheme runs into problems when he introduces the concept of the Subject of knowledge. If he clearly took the position that the Subject is made of Will and that Will itself generates consciousness using the brains of animals and humans, he would have been consistent. Indeed he seems to be suggesting this materialistic explanation of the Subject and its cognizance in several places, especially in the second volume of *The World as Will and Presentation*. However, he also presented with equal emphasis the concept of a cosmic Subject that is not made of Will, and it is this concept that makes it possible for the *purification* of consciousness and the attainment of a will-less state, which are essential for salvation from the suffering of the phenomenal world and egoistic individual existence within it. Obviously, this other view of the Subject as a metaphysical principle independent of Will is not consistent with the purely materialistic view of both objects and subjects. Corresponding to these two metaphysical concepts Schopenhauer portrayed two different pictures of human beings. On one hand he portrayed an individual person as being driven by egoism and sexuality and constantly striving to fulfill selfish desires and eventually suffering; on the other hand, he presented the case of a saintly person who has no ego-sense, is full of compassion for all beings and free of suffering. In the first case the individual is a product of Will, and in the other case the person has escaped the grip of Will and is identified with the pure cognition of the cosmic Subject. This portrayal calls for two different principles operating in a human being — will and will-less pure cognition — and this view is contrary to the claim that the essence of everything is Will. Schopenhauer himself was aware of this inconsistency, and in order to explain that these two subjects are, at least on the individual level, the same, he made the statement that the identity of the self of willing and the Subject of knowledge is "a miracle par excellence". This issue regarding the relation of Schopenhauer's subject of knowledge with Will is fairly complicated. Richard Aquila examined this issue in more detail in the 'Translator's Introduction' of his translation of Schopenhauer's book, *The World as Will and Presentation, Volume One.* (Aquila 2008)

An individual person can transition from the normal state of willing to a will-less state of pure cognition. The will-less state in this case will be free of motivation and desire, but it still is founded on Will because it is a human being that is in this state. This presents a puzzle: how can will remove itself and become will-less? Schopenhauer was aware of this issue and his answer was that will 'turns against itself' when a person truly understands the real cause for suffering, which is individual will. The other alternative that the Subject represents a different metaphysical principle also raises a question: does the Subject represent acts of cognizance without any self or agent associated with it, engaging in those acts, or does it have a being or self associated with it? In the first case the Subject is not any sort of substance or 'thing', spiritual or otherwise. The "one eye looking through many eyes" would simply be whatever cognizance is present when an act of cognizance occurs, and it is expressed through a material medium, which is the brain of an animal or a human being. We may note that it would be contrary to the concept of Self (Atman) of the Upanishads and that of a Conscious Being (Purusha) of Bhagavad Gita, which supposedly influenced Schopenhauer's thinking. The Hindu view of the Self or

Subject is that of a spiritual entity, whose substance is consciousness. (I will discuss this further when I compare Schopenhauer's philosophy with Indian philosophies.) It is quite possible that Schopenhauer was torn between these alternative concepts about the Subject. Unfortunately, he wrote in a way that makes it impossible to conclude that one or the other was his actual view.

## Meaning of Life and Denial of Will

Schopenhauer is considered by many as one of the most pessimistic philosophers of the world. (Tanner, 1999) According to Schopenhauer life does not have any meaning and there is no purpose that Will is trying to fulfill. However, it should not be overlooked that there is a positive side of his philosophy since he recognized that it is possible to deny Will and stop the suffering. Schopenhauer also mentioned at least once that Will is "striving for the highest possible objectification". (Schopenhauer 1819, p. 188). At that level it can generate a distinct knowledge of itself with the consequence of Will turning against itself.

Schopenhauer identified the cause of the suffering to be *individual* will. The universal Will, which is One, becomes many through the principle of individuation (the *principium individuationis*), and this process creates in each individual person the sense of ego and an individual will. In this context Schopenhauer refers to a concept of Hindu philosophy, which is known as Maya, and he equates the principle of individuation with the 'veil of Maya'. (I will examine the concept of Maya in detail in a subsequent section.) Individual will begets selfishness as each individual person competes with others to preserve and promote himself. In Schopenhauer's words,

> every individual, utterly vanishing and diminished to nothing in the boundless world, nonetheless makes himself the center of the world, has regard for his own existence and well-being before any other, indeed, in the natural standpoint, is ready to sacrifice all else to it, is ready to annihilate the world, just to maintain its own self, this drop in the sea, somewhat longer. (Schopenhauer 1819, p. 388)

Further, individual will cannot bring happiness because it is insatiable. Even when a desire is satisfied, the happiness is only temporary as success breeds another desire, which wants satisfaction. Since one cannot have all desires satisfied, even the fulfillment of some desires ultimately ends in disappointment and unhappiness. It should be pointed out that according to some commentators Schopenhauer's Will is intrinsically evil. (Tanner, 1999) However, such an interpretation is not correct. Schopenhauer's Will is a blind striving force, and by itself it is neither good nor evil.

Although Schopenhauer's view of human existence undoubtedly is very pessimistic, gloomy and without reference to any meaningful purpose, he did see and propose a way for salvation, i.e., a way to get out of the suffering. Since the root cause of suffering is individual will, he thought that it is only by the denial or nullification of will and by suppressing selfish desires that one can find happiness and peace. The denial of will in this case should not be interpreted as the elimination of will because that is not possible since everything is constituted by Will, which is the thing-in-itself. What Schopenhauer means by the denial of will is the denial of egoistic feelings which makes one person compete against another. The denial of will by an individual is possible when he is no longer deceived by the 'veil of Maya' and can see what really is going on; however, it is not easy for anyone to deny will. In this context Schopenhauer gave special recognition to artists and ascetic saints. He believed that it is possible for artists and ascetics to attain a level of consciousness where the sense of being a separate individual is transcended, and thereby one can identify with the world as a whole. This concept of the denial of 'will for life' brings out the mystic in Schopenhauer as he writes about overcoming one's separative ego sense and seeing the unity behind diversity. A few examples of his thoughts on this approach to life are given below:

> . . . when that veil of Maya, the *principium individuationis*, is so greatly lifted from the eyes of a person that he no longer makes the egoistic distinction between his own person and others, but participates as much in the suffering of other individuals

> as in his own ....... must also regard the endless suffering of all living things as his own, and so appropriate the entire world's pain. (Schopenhauer 1819, p. 439)

> ... the cognizance of the whole just described, of the essence of things in themselves, becomes the *quieter* of all and every willing. The will now turns away from life; it now shudders before its enjoyments, in which it is cognizant of its affirmation. Man attains to the state of voluntary renunciation, resignation, true composure and complete will-lessness. (Schopenhauer 1819, p. 439-440)

A question that arises in this context is: what can be the leverage that one can use to deny will? There is no place for higher Will in Schopenhauer's philosophy since he is an atheist. What he seems to suggest is that the realization of the fictitious nature of individual ego together with the knowledge of the unity and interconnectedness of all individuals is the liberating force. Further, this liberation from the demands of Will is possible because of his metaphysical view of the universal Subject, which is not constituted by Will. His thoughts on a universal subject, a world-eye looking out from all cognizant beings, are reminiscent of Hindu (Vedanta) philosophy, which we will examine soon. The following passage from his writing reflects this view:

> Just as we earlier saw hate and malice conditioned by egoism and the latter resting on cognizance caught up in the *principium individuationis*, so we found the origin and essence of righteousness — and then, as it is goes further, love and generosity up to their highest degrees — to be penetration of that *principium individuationis*, which alone, insofar as it nullifies the distinction between one's own and other individuals, can render possible and explain that complete goodness of disposition which extends to the point of the most unselfinterested love and most generous self-sacrifice. (Schopenhauer 1819, p. 438-439)

In several other passages Schopenhauer referred to the unself-interested love, which is mentioned in the above quoted passage, as compassion and pure love, which arise when one is fully cognizant of the suffering of others. (Schopenhauer 1819, p. 435-436) This is similar to Buddhist philosophy. Schopenhauer also extolled the virtues of asceticism and the cultivation of equality, or equanimity, in a person's nature. His description of the attitude and outlook of a person who has been successful in denying the demands of individual will is very similar to some of the descriptions of 'a person of steady wisdom' given in Bhagavad Gita in Chapter 2, and it also resembles a person who attains Nirvana of Buddhism while still living in the world. I will write more about these similarities in a later section where I will compare Schopenhauer's philosophy with Hindu and Buddhist philosophies.

## Part II

## Schopenhauer and Indian Philosophies

Indian philosophies include several different philosophies, and these are Hindu, Buddhist, Jain, Carvaka and Ajiva philosophies. Hindu philosophy itself includes the philosophical schools of Samkhya, Yoga, Naya, Vaisheshika, Mimamsa and Vedanta. Schopenhauer had studied the Hindu philosophies of Vedanta and Samkhya, and also Buddhist philosophy. Vedanta philosophy's foundation is based on the Upanishads (800 — 600 BCE) and Gita (400 BCE), and it is significantly different from Buddhism (500 BCE). Vedanta is the most prominent school of philosophy among Hindu schools. The dualistic philosophy of Samkhya influenced Hindu philosophy substantially although there are certain fundamental differences between Samkhya and Upanishads (Vedanta). The developer of Samkhya is sage *Kapila* (600 BCE); however, its concepts and principles were documented by *Ishwara* Krishna at a later date, and this book is known as Samkhya Karika (500 BCE). Schopenhauer was exposed to the Upanishads, Gita and Samkhya Karika.

## Schopenhauer's Acquaintance with Indian Philosophy

Schopenhauer was introduced to Indian philosophies after he had finished his formal education in philosophy and after he had published his doctoral dissertation as a book. Schopenhauer expressed in glowing language how deeply he appreciated and admired the philosophical concepts of Upanishads, and I presented a quotation from his writing about Upanishads in the introductory section of this chapter. In addition to the Upanishads Schopenhauer frequently referred to Bhagavad Gita and Buddhism. Furthermore, a few of his philosophical concepts are similar to those of Samkhya Karika.

Schopenhauer's attention was drawn to Gita and Upanishads by a scholar named Friedrich Majer whom he met at the home of Goethe in Weimar in 1813. Majer was an Orientalist. In addition to the Upanishads, Gita, and Samkhya Karika Schopenhauer read many articles dealing with Hinduism in various journals, which he found in libraries; these include *Das Asiatische Magazin* (The Asiatic Magazine), which contained articles on Hinduism as well as Buddhism.

There is some controversy among scholars as to which Indian philosophy text Schopenhauer read first — the Gita or the Upanishads. One scholar who examined this question in depth came to the conclusion that the first book on Indian philosophy read by Schopenhauer was a translated version of the Gita in German. (App, 2006) The translation in German was done by Friedrich Majer from an English translation done by Charles Wilkins. Later he also read a translation of the Gita done by A. G. Schlegel, which was published in 1823. Although nobody can know with certainty how thoroughly Schopenhauer read the translated versions of the Gita, it has been established, based on his handwritten notes and references that he made in his books, that Schopenhauer read a large part, if not all, of the Gita.

Schopenhauer' read a translation in Latin of some of the Upanishads; this book is known as *Oupnek'hat*, which itself was translated from a translation of the Upanishads in Persian. It is not known exactly how many of the several Upanishads he read and in what degree of detail. However, from the references that he made to these sources in his writings it is evident that he read Chandogya and Brihadaranyaka Upanishads. An example of his familiarity with the famous verses in Chapter 6 of Chandogya Upanishad, in which the concept of Self (Atman) and its immanence in the world were discussed, can be found in the following quotation from Volume One of his book *The World as Will and Presentation*:

> We find the direct depiction in the Vedas, fruit of the highest human cognizance and wisdom, the core of which, in the Upanishads, has finally reached us as the greatest gift of this century, expressed in a variety of ways, but particularly where all the beings of the world, living and lifeless, are led in succession before the gaze of the disciple and over each of them pronounced the word that, become a standard formula, was given the title *Mahavakya*: *Tatoumes*, or more correctly, *tat tvam asi*. It means: "This is you". (Schopenhauer, 1819, p. 413-414)

Comparison of Metaphysical Aspects

The issues or topics that my comparative discussion will focus on include: the world as a presentation of objects to subjects, the thing-in-itself, egoism and veil of Maya, and Will. I will present more comparative analysis later.

The World as a Presentation of Objects to Subjects

One of the fundamental concepts of Schopenhauer's philosophy, which is reflected in the title of his famous book, *The World as Will and Presentation*, has striking similarity with a concept of Samkhya philosophy. This concept is that the phenomenal world is a presentation (*Vorstellung* in German) of objects to cognizant subjects as in a theatrical presentation. Schopenhauer also uses the metaphor of a dream. However, despite this striking similarity between Schopenhauer's philosophy and Samkhya with regard to the concept of objects being presented to subjects, there is a fundamental difference between the two philosophies. Samkhya is a strictly dualistic philosophy as it believes that there are two separate principles operating in the phenomenal world although they are linked together. One of these principles constitutes all objects, which include in addition to objects of gross physical matter many seemingly immaterial things such as life force, mind, ego, and intelligence. This active principle is Nature (*Prakriti* in Sanskrit), which is energy and its process. However, Nature does not possess consciousness, which resides in the other principle with which it is connected. The other principle is Conscious Being or Soul (*Purusha* in Sanskrit), and it is immutable and self-luminous. It should be noted that according to Samkhya, Nature is one but Soul is multiple, i.e., there are numerous individual souls or subjects. It is also important to note that according to Samkhya, Nature's dynamism depends on the presence and consent of Soul which reflects the activities of Nature. The Soul has to be present to observe or witness in order for Nature to become active and make its presentation. The Soul can give or withdraw its consent to the activities of Nature. This is similar to the case of a theatrical presentation or a dream, where spectators must be present for a play or dream to begin and continue. Further, some of the elements of Nature such as intelligence and ego assume the hue of consciousness when their activities are reflected in Soul's consciousness. In Verse 21 of Samkhya Karika the relationship between Nature and Soul is compared to that between a blind person carrying a lame person with unimpaired sight. The blind person in this verse represents the unconscious but active Nature, and the sighted lame person represents the conscious but inactive Soul. Schopenhauer uses the same example or analogy to depict the relation between will and intellect or cognizance. (Schopenhauer, 1844, p.236) Schopenhauer also says that intellect is a product of brain function, which would seem to make it a manifestation of will. It should be noted that there is no universal Subject in Sankhya similar to Schopenhauer's Subject, and that for Sankhya subjects or souls are always multiple and individual.

Whether the dualism of Samkhya is compatible with Schopenhauer's philosophy is a debatable issue. On one hand his philosophy appears to have strong similarity with Samkhya as he presents a dualistic view when he envisions Matter in an undifferentiated state and a universal Subject standing as the two poles of the world as presentation before individual objects and subjects are manifested, and says that it is only in some sort of union of this Matter with the Subject that there comes to be constituted, as objects for the Subject, a world of objects that can be thought of as made of matter. He also clearly says, or implies, in some places that the Subject is not made of Will. On the other hand in some places he seems to present a monistic view when he says that everything including the Subject of pure cognition is constituted of Will. According to this view all states of cognizance are functions of the brain. Actually it may be impossible to resolve this incoherency, and perhaps Schopenhauer is not consistent.

## The Thing-in-Itself in Schopenhauer's and Indian Philosophies

If we interpret Schopenhauer's philosophy as monism of Will, it will agree with the philosophy of the Upanishads (Vedanta) at least in the one respect that everything in the universe is constituted by a single principle. However, this single principle for the Upanishads is Self (Atman) whereas that for Schopenhauer would be Will, and clearly there is a difference between these two principles. Furthermore, for Vedanta there also is another status of Reality beyond Self, and it is Brahman, which is the Absolute. Self is a status of Brahman in relation with the universe. Schopenhauer's philosophy does not accommodate any transcendent reality similar to Brahman. this is because there are fundamental differences between Hinduism's Self (Atman) and Schopenhauer's Will with regard to the thing-in-itself of the empirical world. Self (Atman) is a conscious principle that has a force inherent in it. Force represents its 'becoming' aspect, and simultaneously the consciousness represents the 'being' aspect, which supports the 'becoming' aspect. Schopenhauer's Will basically is a blind force, a dynamic principle, and it represents only 'becoming'. Schopenhauer did not discuss any 'being' aspect of Will underlying or supporting its 'becoming' aspect. Both objects and subjects are made of Will, although, as I said earlier, he presented two types of subjects — the subject of willing and the subject of knowledge. His 'subject of willing' is similar to the 'ego' (*Ahamkara* in Sanskrit) of Hindu philosophy, and Samkhya's too; ego is constituted by Nature (Prakriti). However, the comparison of the concept of Schopenhauer's subject of knowledge with Atman of Hindu philosophy is complicated. There is a similarity between the two and there is a difference too. A few times Schopenhauer described the Subject of knowledge as "one eye" that is present in all cognizant subjects. This is similar to the concept of a universal Self or Conscious Being presented in the Gita's Chapter XIII, which is described as "one knower of the field" present in all individual "fields". (Schopenhauer copied this portion of the text into his notebook.) The Upanishads also present the concept of a universal Self, or Subject, in many ways. Verse III. 7. 23 of Brhadaranyaka Upanishad describes Self as "he who is never perceived, but is the perceiver". Schopenhauer described the Subject as "that which is cognizant, never cognized". (Schopenhauer, 1819, p. 34). Similarities between these two descriptions are obvious. However, whereas for Gita and Upanishads this Self along with its conscious force is the essence, or thing-in-itself, of everything, Schopenhauer's Subject of knowledge seems to be fundamentally distinct from Will, and it is not the essence of everything in the universe. Schopenhauer was ambiguous about how his Subject of knowledge fits in with his view that everything is constituted of Will, and sometimes he seems to say that this 'Subject of knowledge' is same as the 'subject of willing,' or at least he says that subjects of knowledge are instances of Will becoming cognizant. In any case, Schopenhauer never presented the Subject of knowledge as the thing-in-itself, or Self, of everything. It is also likely that Schopenhauer's Subject is not a 'thing' or 'being' similar to the Self (Atman) or Conscious Being (Purusha) of Hindu philosophy. It may very well represent merely conscious acts, or the pure 'form' of conscious acts, without any underlying unitary reality supporting it.

In the context of 'thing-in-itself' I should add that Buddhist philosophy does not recognize any unitary principle or entity as the reality underlying the phenomenal existence. According to Buddhism phenomenal existence is a dynamic process, or flow, consisting of a chain of causally connected events, and there is no substantial entity such as Will or Self underlying this flow.

In early Buddhist philosophy this concept is known as 'No-Self" (Anātman), and in Mahayana Buddhism it was further extended to the concept of 'emptiness' (Sūnyatā). The explanation of 'emptiness' is founded on the principle of 'dependent arising', or 'inter-dependent-origination', according to which no entity has an independent or intrinsic existence since everything is caused by something else. Schopenhauer believed in the law of causality, but he also believed in a thing-in-itself underlying and constituting everything in the phenomenal world. The metaphysical foundation of Buddhism is quite different from that of Schopenhauer's philosophy although there are similarities in some other aspects.

Egoism and Veil of Maya in Schopenhauer's and Indian Philosophies

The description of desire-filled, egoistic, and competitive human psychology that Schopenhauer presents agrees with Hindu and Buddhist views of life for the majority of human beings. Both Hinduism and Buddhism agree with Schopenhauer that the root causes of human suffering are 'ego' and 'desire'. With regard to 'ego', Schopenhauer's view that it is formed only in space and time, which represent the 'principle of individuation' or the '*principium individuationis*' (in Latin), agrees with the views of Vedanta and Samkhya since according to both philosophies ego is a construction of manifested Nature. As Sri Aurobindo explains,

> The formation of a mental and vital ego tied to the body-sense was the first great labour of the cosmic Life in its progressive evolution; for this was the means it found for creating out of matter a conscious individual. (*Synthesis of Yoga*, p. 341)

Schopenhauer attributes the egoistic human psychology to the principle of individuation, which, on several occasions, he equates with 'the veil of Maya'.

> *Maya* for Schopenhauer was the falsification of our perception of the 'world', the taking of the world to be nothing more than a collection of differentiated phenomena and individuals of

heterogeneous natures . . . (Berger, p. 221)

Schopenhauer believed that because of this false perception caused by the veil of Maya people fail to see the unitary and all-pervasive Will operating in the universe and they act egoistically thinking that each individual is a completely separate entity. This interpretation of the word Maya is compatible with the meaning of Maya in Vedanta philosophy although the unitary principle for Vedanta is different. Actually Maya has been used with different meanings in different Hindu scriptures, for example, as a magical power of gods (in Rg Veda), as a power of creating illusion (in certain versions of non-dualistic Vedanta), as the cause of ignorance in lower Nature (in the Gita), and the creative divine force inherent in Self (Atman) or Brahman (in Svetaswatara Upanishad). In the Gita, the word Maya is used only in a few places; in Chapters VII and XVIII where it is used the meaning is similar to how Schopenhauer interpreted it. In verse VII-5 the Gita makes a distinction between two Natures — one higher or supreme (Para Prakriti), and the other lower (Apara Prakriti). The higher is the spiritual Nature beyond the manifested world, and the lower Nature constitutes the phenomenal world. The lower Nature is made up of the three modes of energy (Gunas) — Sattwa, which represents intelligence and purity; Rajas, which represents force and action; and Tamas, which represents inertia and non-intelligence. In Verses VII- 12, 13 and 14 the Gita refers to this lower Nature (Prakriti) as Maya and explains that this lower nature of three Gunas creates a false view of things, bewilders our knowledge, and creates the ego sense. It should be emphasized that the Gita does not view Maya as creating illusion and making an unreal phenomenal existence seem to be real. However, there are certain schools of Vedanta philosophy that consider the phenomenal world created by Maya as illusory or unreal. Schopenhauer did not consider the phenomenal world as unreal, and his interpretation of Maya is consistent with that of the Gita.

<u>Will in Schopenhauer's and Indian Philosophies</u>

Schopenhauer uses the term Will in a very broad sense, and

according to his terminology 'desire' is made of 'Will'. Hindu philosophy, however, makes a distinction between 'desire' and 'will' although these are interrelated. Vedanta philosophy, which is based on the Upanishads, generally agrees with the psychological scheme that Samkhya presents according to which the psychological/psychic forces within a human being are grouped into broad categories in a hierarchical fashion. Starting with the sense capacities (Jnanendriyas in Sanskrit), the next higher group is mind (Manas), then comes 'ego' (Ahamkara), and then intelligence (Buddhi). 'Desire' is generated by the interaction of sense capacities, mind, and ego sense. Hinduism recognizes the pervasive role of desire in ordinary human life. In the words of Sri Aurobindo,

> . . . this desire is essential to the ordinary man; he cannot live or act as an individual without knotting up all his action into the service of some kind of lower or higher craving, preference or passion. (*Synthesis of Yoga*, p. 648)

However, for Hinduism this desire is not synonymous with will. Will in Hinduism is the power of choice and determination to act in order to fulfill a chosen goal, and it has a higher or superior status than desire. Will is included in Buddhi along with intelligence. Buddhi, which is the discriminating power, is the highest principle in Nature. In the Chandogya Upanishad it is said that (Verse VII. 4. 1) 'Will, assuredly, is greater than mind'. The Sanskrit term for will is '*samkalpa*', and that for desire is 'kama'. The psychology of Samkhya agrees with this scheme.

It should be pointed out that for the psychology of Hinduism the different categories of psychic principles such as desire, mind and will are not completely separate entities but represent a continuum, and, furthermore, these can get mixed up with each other. For example, an aspect of will can join desire and strive for its fulfillment. According to Hinduism, in the lower forms of life there may not be a difference between desire and will and these two are fused with each other, but in human beings the difference begins to show, and in spiritual life will plays an important role since it can overcome the compulsive force of desire or craving. Schopenhauer does not make this distinction between 'desire' and 'will' even for human beings, and in his philosophy these two are blended together. Actually Schopenhauer's Will includes a variety of forces including vital or life-force, desire, 'will power' in the sense of the power of choice, and even subconscious and wholly unconscious natural forces. In Hinduism there is also a higher or divine Will, and human will is considered to be a degraded form of the divine Will; but for Schopenhauer, who was an atheist, there is no Divine Being and so the question of a divine Will does not arise. For Buddhism too there is no divine Will.

## Nature of Existence and Purpose of Life in Schopenhauer's and Indian Philosophies

The differences between Schopenhauer's philosophy and Hinduism with respect to metaphysical concepts lead to a major difference in the outlook about the meaning and purpose of life. According to Schopenhauer everything in the phenomenal world is a manifestation of Will, which is a blind force, and there is no reason why this force is manifesting. Furthermore, as I said in an earlier section, according to Schopenhauer human existence must contain suffering, and the primary reason for this suffering is that Will creates a fictitious 'ego sense' in individuals along with individual wills, and the egos of different persons compete against each other. In some contexts Schopenhauer considered this life of suffering so undesirable that he suggested that non-existence of the world is preferable to its existence. For example, in one place he suggested that we can say to a dying person, "You are ceasing to be something it would have been better for you never to have become." (Schopenhauer, 1844, p. 558) Despite his pessimism and dire view of life, Schopenhauer also presented a few positive ideas. One of these ideas is that Will is trying to manifest higher forms of life with greater levels of cognizance. In his own words Will is "striving for the highest possible objectification". (Schopenhauer 1819, p. 188) This idea provides a hint of an evolutionary process, but he did not clearly say what this process could lead to. Moreover, he recognized that when a high level of cognition is attained it is possible for one to deny or nullify Will and reach a state where suffering ceases to exist. However, he presented the attainment of a will-less state of pure cognition merely as a way to end suffering and not as the true meaning and aim of existence.

Hinduism recognizes and agrees with the description of phenomenal human existence that Schopenhauer presented, and it also recognizes that individual ego and its desire are the root causes of suffering of human beings. However, Hinduism disagrees with the premise that suffering is a fundamental characteristic of phenomenal human existence. According to Hinduism suffering is attributable to ignorance about the true Self of everything, which unites diverse individual beings of the world. Furthermore, according to Hindu philosophy one of the fundamental attributes of Self (*Atman*) and the Ultimate Reality (*Brahman*) is delight or bliss. For example, one verse of the Taittiriya Upanishad (Verse II. 7. 1) says, "For, truly, on getting the essence, one becomes blissful. For who, indeed, could live, who breathe, if there were not this bliss in space?" In the same Upanishad another verse (III. 6. 1) says, "He knew that Brahman is bliss. For truly, beings here are born from bliss, when born, they live by bliss and into bliss, when departing, they enter." (Radhakrishnan, 1994) This blissful characteristic of existence, of course, is not evident in everyday life of ordinary human beings; however, according to Hinduism it can be found through spiritual practice. It also can be argued that every experience in the world is not necessarily painful, and that for every case of suffering there can be found one or more cases of happiness.

With regard to the purpose of life in the manifested universe, there are different answers from different schools of thought within Hinduism. The philosophy of Mayavada believes that the world is an illusion, and so getting out of Samsara, i.e., the cycle of birth and rebirth, and merging one's individual consciousness with Brahman, the ultimate 'a-cosmic' Reality, should be the ultimate goal of human beings. For this philosophy there is no teleology or lofty purpose for the existence of this world. For the followers of dualistic Vedanta who practice a devotion-oriented spiritual path

(Bhakti-yoga), the world is a play of the divine, which is referred to as 'Lila' in Sanskrit. This philosophy does not consider the world to be an illusion; however, it envisions another world of eternal beauty and bliss, which lies beyond the phenomenal realm, where the souls of human beings can participate in divine play without the suffering associated with this world. Getting out of *Samsara* by removing the 'veil of Maya' and reaching that other world should be the goals of this life according to this philosophy. Both of these philosophies reject this world, but there are a few other schools of philosophy within Hinduism including Sri Aurobindo's view that believe in the possibility of transformation of human nature and the establishment of a harmonious life on this earth, which will be free from suffering caused by the clash of egoistic personalities. In his book *The Life Divine* Sri Aurobindo's explains the concept of the evolution of consciousness and transformation of human nature. According to him 'Nature' is slowly moving, or evolving, toward the establishment of divine life on earth and the goal of human life should be to participate in this process consciously. (Sri Aurobindo, 1973)

Schopenhauer's view that suffering is a fundamental characteristic of human life has strong similarity with the outlook of Buddhism although the metaphysical structure of Buddhism is different from that of Schopenhauer's philosophy. The first of the four Noble Truths of Buddhism is the Truth of Suffering (*Duhkha*). What this Noble Truth says is that "sooner or later, in some form or another, no matter what they do, beings are confronted by and have to deal with *duhkha*". (Gethin, p. 60) Buddhism also offers an insight to the causes of suffering and a way for the cessation of suffering. Schopenhauer too offers an explanation for suffering and a way to end it. The goal for Buddhists is to get out of the cycle of birth, death and rebirth and attain Nirvana. (Rebirth in this case means the continuation of the causal chain.) The definition of Nirvana is somewhat controversial and its meaning may vary in different contexts. Nirvana can be attained in this life or after death. In the first case, i.e., when one is living, Nirvana means the extinction of all desires and the attainment of perfect equanimity. Nirvana after death can mean either annihilation or a peaceful pure existence, and scholars have different opinions on this issue. Schopenhauer was familiar with the concept of Nirvana and he used this word several times in his writings. However, he did not believe in rebirth either of a soul or in the sense of the continuation of the causal chain of one's individual life; so for him the worthy goal seems to be the attainment of a will-less non-egoistic state of consciousness in this life, which is similar to attaining Nirvana when one is alive in this world.

## Path for Salvation in Schopenhauer's and Indian Philosophies

Schopenhauer wrote in detail about a path for salvation or the ending of suffering, and his recommended approach is remarkably similar to some schools of Hindu philosophy and also of Buddhism. He devoted the Fourth Book of Volume One of his book *The World As Will and Presentation* to this subject, which he called 'affirmation and denial of the will for life'. An example of his thoughts is quoted below:

> . . . when that veil of Maya, the *principium individuationis*, is so greatly lifted from the eyes of a person that he no longer makes the egoistic distinction between his own person and others, but participates as much in the suffering of other individuals as his own, and is thereby not only helpful to the highest degree but even ready to sacrifice his own individual whenever a number of others can thereby be rescued, then it follows of itself that such a person —who recognizes his innermost and true self in all beings — must also regard the endless sufferings of all living things as his own, and so appropriate the entire world's pain. (p. 439)

Hinduism agrees with Schopenhauer completely that it is the sense of ego that makes a person feel separate from others. In Sri Aurobindo's words,

. . . the human or egoistic view is that of a world of innumerable separate creatures each self-existent and different from the others, each trying to get its utmost possible profit out of the others and the world. (Sri Aurobindo, *The Upanishads*, 1981, p. 48)

Hinduism also believes that the ego is a temporary construction of Nature and that a person can get release from its grip by appropriate spiritual practice. Further, when a person is able to loosen the grip of ego, he can find his true essence or self, and then he gains a different outlook and sees that there is a universal Self connecting all individuals. This realization is an essential step toward gaining spiritual liberation. The following verse from Isha Upanishad conveys this concept.

> Isha 7. When, to one who knows, all beings have, verily, become one with his own self, then what delusion and what sorrow can be to him who has seen this oneness?

The difference between Schopenhauer and Vedanta philosophy is that the unifying principle for Schopenhauer is Will, whereas for Vedanta it is spiritual consciousness (Self), and this is a major difference. Schopenhauer's philosophy does include the concept of a cosmic Subject, which is very similar to Vedanta's Self, and it seems that salvation would have to lie for Schopenhauer in one's identifying with, or becoming, that Subject and not in becoming one with some sort of undifferentiated oneness of Will.

Besides breaking through the veil of Maya and recognizing that the same universal Will is functioning in each individual, Schopenhauer recommends that a person seeking salvation and the end of suffering must deny individual will to operate in himself. Schopenhauer seems to be thinking of a sincere and thorough recognition of the oneness of everything and not just in an intellectual or abstract way. He then goes on to discuss in detail the practice of asceticism as a virtue, and he gives examples of ascetic practices in Christianity and also Hinduism. He also discusses mysticism and in particular refers to the German mystic Meister Eckhart. With reference to the writings of Christian saints and mystics he writes,

> These preach, besides purest love and utter renunciation, to-

> tal voluntary poverty, true composure, complete indifference in the face of all worldly things, dying away from one's own will and rebirth in God, total forgetting of one's own person and becoming immersed in the perception of God. (Schopenhauer, 1819, p. 449)

Schopenhauer's idea of the denial of will raises a question about the agent that is needed to deny 'will' since it is doubtful that it makes sense to suppose that the 'will' itself will want to deny itself. Schopenhauer himself was aware of this issue, and he dealt with it in two different ways. First, he said that when a person is able to penetrate the 'veil of Maya' and "no longer makes the egoistic distinction between his own person and others", he becomes very compassionate towards others, and "his will turns around, no longer affirms its own essence, mirrored in the phenomenon, but denies it." (Schopenhauer, 1819, p. 439-440) The other way that this liberation from the demands of Will is possible is linked with his metaphysical view of the universal Subject, which is not constituted by Will.

Schopenhauer's approach to salvation and the ending of suffering is similar to the Buddhist approach. Buddha emphasized that one must rely on oneself and not depend on receiving help from other sources. For Buddhism there is no God, or a higher divine Will, to rely on. For Vedanta too a sincere and firm resolve is necessary for breaking out of the grip of 'ego'. However, for theistic schools of Vedanta reliance on divine guidance and grace is also recommended. The giving up of ego sense and attachment to worldly things of pleasure is fundamental to both Buddhist and Hindu spiritual practices.

As discussed earlier, Hinduism makes a distinction between desire and will, and it prescribes the denial of desire and not the denial of will as a way to alleviate suffering. In both Hinduism and Buddhism the main cause of human suffering is identified as desire, which arises from a person's ego. In the Katha Upanishad it is said (Verse II.3.14) that "when all desires that dwell within the human heart are cast away, a mortal becomes immortal and (even) here he attains to Brahman". Bhagavad Gita recommends a step by step approach. Gita's first step is to act without allowing the 'fruits of action' to be the motive. (Verse II. 47). It is only in an advanced stage of spiritual practice that the denial of one's own initiative for actions is prescribed. Gita (Verse XII. 16) recommends that a spiritual aspirant be *sarvarambha parityagi* (in Sanskrit), or in other words recommends that one should give up all initiative for actions. In *Katha* Upanishad the Verse I. 2. 20 says, "the unstriving man (*a-kratu*) beholds Him (Self), and becomes freed from sorrow". It should be noted that giving up initiative for actions does not mean complete inaction. What is recommended is to give up one's own choice of work and seek higher guidance to direct one's actions. In Schopenhauer's approach there is no higher guidance for directing one's actions. For Schopenhauer there is only a *universal* Will, i.e., the one Will, which is manifested in all entities in the phenomenal world. But there is no reason, in Schopenhauer's philosophy, for considering it of 'higher' nature than individual wills. If anything, it seems, what is truly 'higher' can only be the state of pure will-less cognizance, which is the characteristic of the one Subject. Unfortunately, as we have seen, the status of the Subject is particularly unclear in his thinking.

**Concluding Remarks**

Schopenhauer is widely known for his pessimistic view of human life. This is somewhat unfortunate because it covers up several other aspects of his philosophy, which are very attractive. He was a maverick in the group of German philosophers of his time which included eminent philosophers like Johann G. Fichte, Friedrich W. J. Schelling, and George W. F. Hegel. Schopenhauer did not receive adequate recognition during the early part of his career, and he was somewhat frustrated for that reason. It is only much later that he received accolades from other philosophers and intellectuals. Eventually he left a deep impression on several philosophers and intellectuals who followed him, and perhaps the most famous among them is Friedrich Nietzsche (1844 — 1900). Nietzsche in the beginning was very impressed with Schopenhauer, but later he openly rejected some his premises. Another great philosopher of the twentieth century who was influenced by Schopenhauer is Ludwig Wittgenstein. Carl Jung, the famous psychiatrist, also was impressed with Schopenhauer's thoughts on the 'subconscious' aspects of human psychology. In addition to philosophers and psychologists Schopenhauer's writings inspired several famous artists, musicians and literary persons. I must point out that this article is of limited scope and that I did not present any discussion on Schopenhauer's extensive thoughts on aesthetics, music and art.

Schopenhauer did not like speculative philosophies and he tried to develop a very realistic and, as he believed, empirically grounded explanation of phenomenal existence. His analysis of human psychology and behaviour is very realistic and his description of human behavior deserves a lot of credit. Commentators differ as to how 'metaphysical' his view of one Will is. But he also introduced the concept of the cosmic Subject, which not only seems very metaphysical but also seems to have created some incoherency in his metaphysical scheme. On the other hand, it enabled him to present a way out of the grip of Will. The description of his approach to ending suffering is powerful and a great contribution not only to philosophy but also to literature. There is a mystical aspect of his philosophy, which is revealed when he describes how a will-less person goes beyond his selfish ego and identifies with everything in the world. The concept of a universal/cosmic Subject of knowledge also has a mystical aspect. Unfortunately this aspect is often overlooked.

With regard to the impact of Indian philosophies on Schopenhauer, he himself acknowledged that he was deeply influenced by the Upanishads. His writings have numerous references to the Upanishads, the Bhagavad Gita and the Puranas as well as Hindu customs. He also made several references to concepts of Buddhist philosophy. There are some scholars who are of the opinion that Schopenhauer did not understand Hindu philosophy. I disagree with this view. In my assessment he had a clear understanding of the basic tenets of Hindu philosophies based on Samkhya Karika as well as Upanishads and the Gita. During his time translations of Indian spiritual texts were rare. Despite the limited access to publications on Indian philosophies Schopenhauer made a sincere effort to read as well as collect literature on Indian philosophies. His explanation of 'tat tvam asi', or 'that thou art', which he presented in Volume One of his book *The World as Will and Presentation* is very clear and accurate. (Schopenhauer, 1819, p. 413-414) (I presented a quotation on this earlier.) His description of the Subject as "that which is cognizant of all things and of which none is cognizant" is clearly similar to the description of Self in Brhadaranyaka Upanishad. Further, one of his favorite descriptions of the Subject as "the world's *one eye* that looks out from all cognizant beings" is similar to that of the universal Purusha (Conscious Being) given in the Gita — 'the Knower of the Field in all Fields'. His understanding of the concept of Maya also is fine. Some aspects of his philosophy have strong similarities with Samkhya Karika, and some others with the Upanishads; but he did not incorporate either school of thought fully into his philosophy. He made inconsistent statements about the relation of Will with the pure Subject of cognition. In some places he said that the Subject is will-less, which implies that it is a different principle from Will. This dualistic view is similar to that of Samkhya although there are differences between the two in some detailed aspects. At some other places he seemed to say that Will is the thing-in-itself of everything including the pure Subject of cognition. This latter view is very materialistic. In any case, this incoherency in his own metaphysical scheme does not necessarily indicate that he did not understand Indian philosophies.

Despite his pessimistic view of life Schopenhauer presented a way to end suffering, and his approach to salvation is very similar to that of some schools of Hindu philosophy as well as Buddhism. At the core of this approach is the denial of Will, which leads to a will-less state of pure cognition combined with compassion, and this state is similar to the experience of Self (Atman) of the Upanishads and the attainment of Nirvana of Buddhism. Before concluding it would, therefore, be appropriate to read a powerful description of the will-less state of pure cognition given by Schopenhauer:

> But if we turn our gaze from our own neediness and involvement toward those who have overcome the world, in whom the will, having attained to full self-cognizance, recognizes itself in all things and then freely denies itself, and which then only awaits sight of the vanishing of its last trace, along with the body that it animates, then instead of unresting press and drive, instead of constant passage from desire to fear and from joy to sorrow, instead of the never satisfied and never perishing hope in which the dreaming life of the willing human being consists, we are shown that peace which is higher than all reason, that complete stillness of the sea of the spirit, that deep repose, unshakeable confidence, and cheerfulness whose mere reflection in a countenance, such as Raphael and Correggio have depicted it, is an entire sure gospel: only cognizance has remained and the will has vanished. (Schopenhauer, 1819, p. 477)

Finally I would like to add that in my humble opinion Schopenhauer's philosophy deserves more attention from students of philosophy especially in India. One does not have to agree with everything he said, but there is lot to learn from his writings. My study of Schopenhauer's philosophy has been a very rewarding experience, and in the future I hope to write more on some of the aspects of his philosophy that I did not cover adequately in this article.

**Acknowledgement**

This article would not have been possible for me to write without the encouragement and guidance of Dr. Richard E. Aquila, Professor of Philosophy, at the University of Tennessee, Knoxville, Tennessee, USA. He not only introduced me to Schopenhauer, but he read and corrected my writings many times during the preparation of the article and its revised form. The primary sources of literature for this article were the two books of Schopenhauer (The World as Will and Presentation) that he translated from German to English. (Please refer to the list of references for these two books.) I am grateful to Dr. Aquila for his help.

## References

App, Urs (2006), "Schopenhauer's Initial Encounter with Indian Thought", *Schopenhauer-Jahrbuch* 87, 35-76, Königshausen & Neumann.

Aquila, Richard, "Translator's Introduction" in Arthur Schopenhauer: The World as Will and Presentation, Volume One, Pearson Education, Inc., 2008

Berger, Douglas L., *The Veil of Maya: Schopenhauer's System and Early Indian Thought*, Global Academic Publishing, Binghamton University, NY, 2004

Gethin, Rupert, *The Foundations of Buddhism*, Oxford University Press, 1998

Janaway, Christopher, *Schopenhauer: A Very Short Introduction*, OXFORD University Press, 2002.

King, Richard, *Indian Philosophy: An Introduction to Hindu and Buddhist Thought*, Edinburgh University Press, 1999

Mann, Thomas, *The Living Thoughts of Schopenhauer*, David McKay Company, 1939

Nicholls, Moira (1999), "The Influence of Eastern Thought on Schopenhauer's Doctrine of the Thing-in-Itself", *The Cambridge Companion to Schopenhauer*, Edited by Christopher Janaway, Cambridge University Press, (P. 171 — 212)

Radhakrishnan, Sarvepalli, and Moore, Charles. A., *A Source Book in Indian Philosophy*, Princeton University Press, 1957

Radhakrishnan, S., *The Principal Upanishads*, HarperCollins Publisher India, 1994

Schopenhauer, Arthur (1851), *Parerga and Paralipomena*, Volume 2, Translated by E. F. J. Payne, Clarendon Press, 1974

Schopenhauer, Arthur (1819), *The World as Will and Presentation*, Volume One, Translated by Richard E. Aquila, Pearson Longman, 2008 (This translation by Aquila is based on the third edition of the book published in 1859. The original Volume One was published in 1819.)

Schopenhauer, Arthur (1844), *The World as Will and Presentation*, Volume Two, Translated by David Carus and Richard E. Aquila, Prentice Hall, 2010

Sri Aurobindo (1968), *The Foundations of Indian Culture*, Sri Aurobindo Ashram Trust

Sri Aurobindo (1972), *The Synthesis of Yoga*, Sri Aurobindo Ashram Trust

Sri Aurobindo (1972), *The Essays on The* Gita, Sri Aurobindo Ashram Trust

Sri Aurobindo (1973), *The Life Divine*, Sri Aurobindo Ashram Trust

Sri Aurobindo (1981), *The Upanishads*, Sri Aurobindo Ashram Trust

Swami Vivekananda, *The Complete Works of Swami Vivekananda*, Vol. III, Vedanta Press and Bookshop, Calcutta, 1947

Tanner, Michael, *Schopenhauer*, *Routledge*, NY, 1999

# Chapter 5

# Philosophy of Immortality and Rebirth: Western and Eastern Views

## Introduction

Most of us wonder about life after death and we have a variety of questions in our minds. Will I continue to exist after I die in some form? What kind of a world is it where I will go? If I am reborn in this world will it occur immediately after I die, or will I spend some time in another world before the next birth? We also wonder about our existence prior to our birth. If I have a soul that will survive the death of my body, did it exist before my body was formed in my mother's womb? There are also questions about rewards and punishment from God, or the consequences of actions (*Karma*) which may be carried over to after-life. The answers to these questions that common persons accept are largely influenced by their social and religious background. For example, most Hindus believe in life after death and also in rebirth. Most Christians and Jews believe in life after death but not in rebirth. Many Christians believe in something that they call being "born again", but it is a purely *spiritual* rebirth, not life in a physically new body. There are also many very intelligent and highly educated persons in both western and eastern cultures who do not believe in life after death, and some of them think that the belief in the concepts of the immortality of souls and rebirth can be attributed to the fear of the believers to accept 'nothingness' as the state that they will reach after death. In this article I will examine views of major western and eastern religions and also those of a few prominent theologians and philosophers on these questions and issues.

## Concepts and Issues Related to Souls, Immortality, and Rebirth

Before we begin to examine the views of a few famous philosophers and theologians of different religions we should examine certain concepts and issues related to the definition of a soul and also what is meant by immortality and rebirth since these terms are used with different meanings in different cultures and by different writers. There is a variety of notions about what is meant by the term soul. It is generally recognized by all that a human being consists of a gross physical body, which can be touched and felt like matter as we ordinarily think of it, and in this body reside a variety of forces, which include life or vital energy, feelings and emotions, and also mind and intellect. Generally a person who believes in the concept of a soul of some type thinks that the vital, emotional and mental forces residing in his body together constitute his soul and that all these elements are immaterial or incorporeal and can survive after death. On the other hand, materialists believe that all these forces — vital, emotional and mental — are subtle forms of matter and entirely dependent on the physical body. So according to their view, when the body dies these forces dissipate and do not remain in any integrated form. Now, in between these two extreme positions there are views that consider only one or two of these forces to constitute the immaterial soul, and there has been much debate on this issue in western philosophy. Some western philosophers consider mind, or only a certain element of mind such as the intellect, as immaterial or as an immaterial part of a soul. Some others think of mind and emotion together in this way.

There is also an issue related to the concepts of individual and universal souls. Some philosophers believe in individual souls and also in a universal soul, whereas some philosophers do not believe in individual souls but believe in a universal soul. According to the latter view the universal soul generates a sense of an individual self in a person's consciousness by coming in contact with the body and other forces operating in it, but this individual self really is fictitious. In the case of a real individual soul a fundamental question is: Is the individual soul, however it may be defined, a self-subsisting entity that is separable from the body? Another question is: If the soul is separable from the body and survives after death, does it maintain its individuality after death, or does the principle (or, substance) of the soul merge with the universal source of the same principle and lose its individuality? We will return to these concepts when we will examine the views of a few eminent philosophers and theologians of the east and the west.

With regard to immortality the views of common people as well as philosophers and theologians vary. Some believe that the only immortality we can hope for is in the memory of other persons — friends, relatives and others — depending on what we do during our life time. At the other extreme there is a belief in certain religions that not only our soul will survive but that there also will be a resurrection of the body in the sense that a person's dead body will be restored in its living form by God's grace. Some philosophers and theologians believed that only a special faculty of our mind that is acquired by special effort can survive without the body. So they think that every person cannot attain immortality since everyone does not acquire this special faculty.

Some religions believe that a soul is created for the first time when a person is born but it continues to exist after death, whereas some other religions and philosophers believe in the pre-existence of a soul and that a soul is reborn again and again. There is another issue related to the rebirth of a soul and it involves the question whether a soul is reborn in a new body immediately after death. The concept of immediate rebirth is usually called 'transmigration'. However, there are many who believe that a soul stays in other worlds for a long time before it is reborn. Sri Aurobindo preferred to use the term 'rebirth' since it is simple and does not imply the return of a soul either immediately after death or after an interval. (The Problem of Rebirth, p. 9)

## Western Religions and Theologies

In this section I will discuss the views of three religions of the western world — Judaism, Christianity and Islam — and a few western theologians. In the section that will follow this section I will cover the views of western philosophers.

### *Judaism*

Jewish religion presents a few different views on immortality as well as reincarnation. Judaism is focused on life here and now rather than on the afterlife, and that may be one of the reasons why there is a lack of definitive answers to questions about life after death and reincarnation. Theological views range from various interpretations of the Hebrew Bible (*Tanakh*) at one end to the mystical views of Kabbalah and Hasidism at the other end. In between are the Rabbinic views, which are varied since those developed over many years during the early centuries of the Common Era (after Christ) and in several different places where Jewish diasporas existed.

The Hebrew Bible, *Tanakh*, is inconsistent about the immortality of souls and what happens after one dies. Torah, which represents the major portion of *Tanakh*, does not say anything about what happens after a person dies. In Ketuvim, which is included in *Tanakh* but is not a part of Torah, there are a few statements about life after death. With regard to how a human body and soul come into existence, both Judaism and Christianity accept the view of Genesis, which is expressed in Verse 2: 7: "And the Lord God formed man of the dust of the ground, and breathed into his nostrils the breath of life; and man became a living being." According to this verse the soul of a person is created when his body is formed. However, there is no unanimous agreement in Judaism as to exactly when a soul joins a body — whether at conception, or at birth, or at any other time. Generally it is accepted that the ensoulment of a fetus occurs at birth. It is clear that the prior existence of a soul is ruled out.

The verse 2:7 of Genesis has been interpreted by some Jewish theologians as implying that body and soul are a unified entity, and so when the body dies the soul also dies. Further, in Genesis 3: 19 God said to Adam, "For dust you are, and to dust you shall return." This verse also indicates that there is no life after death. However, the more widely accepted view among followers of Judaism is that body and soul are two different entities and that the soul is incorporeal and can survive without the body. This view is supported by a few verses of the Books of Ecclesiastes and Daniel, which are included in Ketuvim and came much later than Genesis. For example, the Verse 12.7 of Ecclesiastes says that after death, "Then the dust will return to the earth as it was, and the Spirit will return to God who gave it." This verse has been interpreted to mean that the human soul is immortal, and it also has been interpreted as ruling out the possibility of the resurrection of the old body. The verse 12.2 of the Book of Daniel also refers to life after death.

Jewish theological views about life after death developed in several stages. During the early stages prior to the Rabbinic stage, the Sadducees, who were the noble priests of the Temple, did not believe in an afterlife whereas the Pharisees, the predecessors of the Rabbis, believed in life after death. In Rabbinic Judaism it is commonly believed that the soul of a person is immortal, and that after death of the body the soul goes to either the Garden of Eden, which is similar to Paradise, or Gehinnom, which is similar to Hell, depending on what the person does during his life time. [I should point out that there are a few other terms used for referring to places where a soul goes to after death, and these are Sheol and Olam Haba.] Many Jewish philosophers and theologians did not accept the common notions of Garden of Eden and Gehinnom. It also should be noted that although the immortality of soul has been accepted in Judaism gradually, there still are many who believe differently. Some are of the opinion that the only type of immortality one can have is through the memories of other persons and the results of one's actions.

The notion of the resurrection of the body some time after death has not been widely accepted in Judaism, and the reincarnation of a soul in a different body also is not accepted widely in traditional Judaism. However, it should not be overlooked that there are some persons of Jewish faith who believe in the concept of resurrection. It is interesting to note that reincarnation is accepted by the mystical versions of Judaism -- Kabbalah and Hasidism. Both Isaac Luria, one of the famous teachers of Kabbalah, and Israel ben Eliezer (also known as Baal Shem Tov), who is considered as the founder of Hasidism, believed in reincarnation. There is considerable discussion within Kabbalah as to which aspect of the soul goes through reincarnation, and it is generally believed that only the lower aspects of the soul — *nefesh* and *ruah* — are reborn in a new body, but *neshamah*, the higher and divine aspect, goes back to God.

*Christianity*

Christianity is largely based on the New Testament, but some of its views including that of the creation of the world and human soul are based on the Hebrew Bible. Christians believe in the verse of Hebrew Bible (Genesis 2: 7), which says: "And the Lord God formed man of the dust of the ground, and breathed into his nostrils the breath of life; and man became a living being." This verse is interpreted in a dualistic manner. It is widely accepted by Christian theologians and common persons that the body is matter but the human soul, which is created by God when the body of a child is formed, is incorporeal and spiritual. The issue of when exactly a soul joins a body is an important moral issue. Commonly it is accepted that human life begins at conception, and so abortion is generally condemned by many Christian denominations. However, this is a controversial issue as some Christians believe that a soul joins a body at birth or at some other stage of the developing fetus.

With regard to the status of the body and soul after death two beliefs are fundamental to most Christians, and these are the immortality of souls and resurrection of bodies. Christian theologians of early centuries after Christ, who are also known as the Church Fathers, discussed these beliefs in their writings extensively. Saint Augustine (354—430) may be included in this group of theologians. To the Fathers of the Church, as Prof. Wolfson pointed out, "the belief that Jesus rose on the third day after crucifixion meant that his soul survived the death of the body and was reinvested with his risen body. Similarly the belief that in the end of days there will be a general resurrection of the dead meant the reinvestment of surviving souls with risen bodies." (Wolfson, 1965, p. 70) The Church Fathers also believed that "in the interval between death and resurrection, the soul had a life of its own without a body, though there was some difference of opinion as to what was the state of the soul's life during that interval." (Wolfson, 1965, p. 70) The Gospels of the New Testament have abundant reference to the belief that one's soul can gain salvation and immortality through Jesus Christ by the grace of God.

The idea of the immortality of souls is more widely accepted by Christian theologians than the concept of the resurrection of a dead body. The concept of resurrection was challenged by many philosophers of ancient and modern times. Some Christian theologians believe that the concept of the resurrection of a body really refers to the formation of a spiritual body for the soul and not the body of flesh and blood. Details of the arguments for and against resurrection are beyond the scope of this article. For our purpose it may be noted that the habitation of a soul in a resurrected body is the closest that an orthodox Christian comes to the idea of rebirth. Those who considered the possibility of rebirth in its true sense of a soul returning to earthly life in a new body formed in the womb of a woman are outside the mainstream of Christians. The Gnostics and some of the early Christians believed in reincarnation, but later on the Church removed such a view.

*Islam*

The most common view among the Muslims about human souls is based on the Quran, and it is that a human being has an immortal soul and there is life after death. It is also believed that there will be a Day of Judgment when God, Allah, will decide whether a person's soul will go to heaven or hell based on what he/she did during his life on the earth. Nobody except God knows when exactly the Day of Judgment will occur, and there is not any clear idea given in Quran as to what happens to the departed souls during the waiting period between death and the Day of Judgment. The common idea among Muslims about a soul is that it is identical to a person's current personality. Rebirth of souls is not accepted in traditional Islam.

There are several Islamic scholars who studied western philosophy and were influenced by Plato and Aristotle. These philosophers include Al-Kindi (800—870), Ibn Sina (980-1037) and Ibn Rushd (1126-98). [Ibn Sina and Ibn Rushd are also known as Avicenna and Averroes respectively.] Their views challenged many of the traditional views of Islam based on the Quran. Their concept of a soul was different from that of common Muslims. In general their philosophies distinguished between a part of consciousness that is intimately connected with the physical body and another part that is rational. They considered the rational part of mind as incorporeal and thought that only this part of mind can be immortal.

Islamic philosophy includes a mystical dimension known as Sufism. In some respects the views of Sufi mystics have similarities with the views of Kabbalah of Judaism and Hinduism since they believe in the concept of a universal soul and the unity of all existing beings. The spiritual practices of Sufis are somewhat different from traditional Muslims. With regard to rebirth of souls Sufis are divided in their views. Certain groups, or orders, of Sufis believe in rebirth; but there are also many Sufis who accept the traditional views of Islam and do not believe in reincarnation.

**Western Philosophers**

In eastern culture there is considerable overlap between religion and philosophy; or in other words, the difference between philosophy and theology, or religious beliefs, is not that great and many philosophical concepts come from religious texts. However, that is not the case for western philosophy and theology. Western philosophers usually do not base their philosophical views on religious scriptures such as the Bible, Torah, or Quran although many of them are religious minded in their personal life. Some of the famous western philosophers belonged to ancient times before these scriptures were written. Theologians base their views primarily on the interpretation of religious scriptures, but they also try to reconcile the differences between the views of scriptures and philosophy. In the previous section I discussed the views of western religions, and in this section I will discuss the views of a few famous western philosophers.

There are a few philosophers in the west who believe in the immortality of souls as well as reincarnation, but their number is small and most of them belonged to the ancient era. One of the earliest philosophers who believed in reincarnation of souls is Pythagoras (570 BC — 495 BCE). Pythagoras believed that the human soul is immortal and that it returns to life again and again in animal as well as human forms. The most famous among philosophers who believed in the immortality of souls and their rebirth is Plato (427 BCE — 347 BCE). Plato's student Aristotle (384 BCE

— 322 BCE) disagreed with his teacher on this issue and some others. Plato's and Aristotle's views have had immense influence on many philosophers and theologians of all three major western religions — Christianity, Judaism, and Islam, and therefore, it would be worthwhile to review their thoughts briefly.

Plato was a dualist. He believed that everything in the world that we experience with our senses is mutable and in some sense merely an appearance. He also believed that there is a reality that transcends the world of the senses and it is where the immutable Forms of the mutable things of the world reside. With regard to the soul of a human being Plato wrote about his concept of what it is in his famous books *Phaedo*, *The Republic*, and *Timaeus*. He believed in reincarnation and his concept is referred to as "metempsychosis". In *The Republic* Plato identified three parts of the human soul — reason or intelligence, appetite, and spirit (or emotion). Appetite is primarily concerned with food, drink and sex. Spirit is a motivating force and it generally accounts for self-assertion and ambition. Reason or intelligence is the part of the soul that is attached to knowledge and truth. These three parts of the soul do not always act in harmony with each other, and it is the rational part that tries to keep the other two parts in control. To explain the relation of the three parts of a soul Plato used his famous allegory of a rider of a chariot trying to control two horses pulling the chariot. The chariot is the soul, the rider represents intelligence or reason, and the two horses represent appetite and spirit (or emotion). The rider is not always able to control the two horses, and similarly the rational part, i.e., intelligence, also is not always successful in controlling appetite and spirit. Individual persons' souls are different according to the dominance of one part over the other two. Some souls are dominated by reason, some by the spirited element and others by bodily appetites. In *Phaedo* Plato discussed what happens to each of these types of souls after death.

According to Plato the tripartite soul of a person is immaterial and can be separated from the body. The soul is reborn several times allowing the possibility of strengthening the rational part and purifying the lower parts. At the ideal limit the rational part of the soul takes over the transformed lower parts, and, if so, at the end of its final reincarnation the soul as a whole goes to the higher world of unchanging realities (or Forms) and lives there forever. Plato also believed that if the lower elements of the soul of a person could not be transformed and integrated with the rational part even after several rounds of reincarnation, those parts would go to an underworld of some type and remain there, while the higher rational part by itself would go to the higher realm of unchanging Forms. [It should be acknowledged that Plato was not very clear as to whether the rational part can go to the higher realm by itself when the lower elements go to an underworld.]

Aristotle did not agree with all aspects of Plato's views although he was his student. Like Plato Aristotle too presented a detailed account of various aspects of human soul, and his views on the relationship of soul and body and immortality of soul were different from Plato's. According to him soul is the animating principle, which he called the 'form' of a body, *qua* living being. To this extent he can be said to agree with Plato, at least with reference to Plato's view of ordinary life. However, Aristotle regarded the soul as more unified with the body than Plato did, and as unable to have a life apart from the body. So based on this view the soul will perish when the body dies. However, Aristotle is more clear in his view that the soul perishes with the body with reference to plants and animals than with reference to human beings, and it is also possible that his stated views were not fully consistent. With regard to the intellect of a human being, he distinguished between a passive part and an active part, and he suggested that the active (or creative) part of intellect is not corporeal and in some sense can not only be separated from the body, but can even be said to exist apart from the body during normal lifetime. The active part of intellect is divine in character and it will not perish with the body at death while the passive part will perish. However, in Aristotle's view the active, or creative, intellect of a person, which survives death, does not have a personal identity and it continues to exist as part of some eternal and unchanging substance, which Aristotle referred to as pure 'actuality' and also as God. (Aristotle's concept of God is different from Judeo-Christian concept of God.)

The famous philosopher Rene Descartes (1596 — 1650) believed in the immortality of individual souls, which he came to prefer to call "minds." He is famous for his philosophy of substance dualism of mind and body. According to Descartes mind and body are made of two different things, which he called 'substances', and they are separable. He, therefore, believed that mind, or soul, can survive the death of body. For Descartes the mind includes self-awareness and also, at least during normal lifetime, sensations and feelings, at least insofar as they are conscious. However, unlike Plato and Aristotle, he did not believe that the mind's attachment to the body is what constitutes the life, or vital force, which animates a body. The latter according to Descartes is purely a question of physiology.

Baruch Spinoza (1632 — 1677), a famous Jewish philosopher, disagreed with the dualism of Plato and Descartes. His views were very different from those of traditional western religions and philosophies. His views were so radically different from the prevailing views of his time that he was excommunicated from the Jewish community by fellow Jews. He believed not only that mind and body are aspects or dimensions of the same substance but also that everything in the world exists as aspects or dimensions of this same substance, which he called God. Spinoza's philosophy recognized matter and mind as "attributes" of God alone, and particular forms of matter and particular minds are only "modes" of those attributes. Spinoza did not believe in the concept of an immortal soul in the way that Plato and Descartes did. According to him many faculties of mind such as imagination and memory do not survive the death of the body. However, he acknowledged an immortal principle or faculty within human beings. In his famous book *Ethics* (Part V, Proposition 23) he wrote, "the human mind cannot be absolutely destroyed with the body, but something of it remains, which is eternal". This 'something' of mind that survives death is related to the essence of mind, and according to Spinoza this essence is knowledge. Spinoza wrote about three different grades of knowledge and believed that only the knowledge of the highest grade makes a portion of mind immortal. However, scholars generally regard Spinoza as denying that there is anything personal and individual about the immortality in question.

An exception is Wolfson, who argued that according to Spinoza "the thought element of the mind that survives death bears the particular characteristics of the individual during his lifetime". (*The Philosophy of Spinoza*, Volume II, p. 295)

There are a few western philosophers, besides Plato, who recognized the existence of a realm altogether beyond the phenomenal world and also believed in an aspect of human beings belonging to this realm. Immanuel Kant (1724 — 1804) and Arthur Schopenhauer (1788 — 1860) are examples. Schopenhauer took a particular interest in Hindu and Buddhist philosophies. Schopenhauer was greatly impressed by the concepts of Upanishads, but he did not acknowledge immortality of individual souls as described in the Upanishads. In his famous book, *The World as Will and Representation*, he postulated two different types of subjects or selves. One is his 'subject of will', which is similar to Indian philosophy's 'ego' (*Ahamkara*). This self is corporeal and so it perishes with the body. His individual subject of knowledge also is constituted by will and perishable. However, he presented the concept of the 'Subject of knowledge', and it is similar in concept to the Self (*Atman*) of Upanishads. He described this Subject as "the world's one eye that looks out from all cognizant beings." This Subject is universal and not individual. Schopenhauer was not clear as to the relationship of the 'Subject of knowledge' with Will, but according to him the Subject is outside space and time and is imperishable. So although he did not acknowledge the immortality of individual subjects, he acknowledged that by the denial of Will one can experience the status of the universal Subject, which is not touched by birth and death. Schopenhauer also believed that Will in its essence as the thing-in-itself is non-perishable. One writer and poet whom Schopenhauer admired is Johann Wolfgang von Goethe (1749 -1832). Goethe believed in reincarnation of souls. There are a few western essayists, poets, scientists, and psychiatrists of the modern era who also believed in reincarnation. They include Ralph Waldo Emerson, Albert Schweitzer, Benjamin Franklin, and Carl Jung. Some of these individuals were clearly influenced by Indian philosophy.

The fundamental reason why most of the modern western

philosophers do not believe in the immortality of souls and reincarnation is because they believe in materialism, or physicalism, according to which all components of the phenomenal world are composed of matter and that there is nothing beyond the physical world. According to them the emergence of vital force, or life, in matter is accidental. They also believe that all of our experiences such as feelings, thoughts, and ideas, which we usually consider to be non-material, actually are subtle forms of matter and can be explained by processes of brain and changes in the neural network. So for materialists who do not believe that any part of our conscious being can survive physical body's death, the question of rebirth does not even arise. In Sri Aurobindo's words, "Rebirth is for the modern mind no more than a speculation and a theory; it has never been proved by the methods of modern science or to the satisfaction of the new critical mind formed by a scientific culture." (The Philosophy of Rebirth, p. 9 — 10) Besides materialism there is also a theory that accepts a vital or life force, as the primary principle, which is manifesting in different forms including matter and mind. The vitalistic view too does not admit the presence of souls that can survive the death of gross bodies. At the best these materialistic and vitalistic theories accept that some of the physical and mental characteristics can be transmitted by parents to their children in the form of chromosomes and genes, and thus some characteristics of the parents continue to exist after their death.

## Views of Eastern Philosophies and Religions

Among the eastern philosophies and religions the two that are most prominent and considered as world religions are Hinduism and Buddhism. Each of these includes several variations of thought and views with regard to souls and rebirth. In this article I will cover only the major schools of Buddhism and Hinduism — Theravada Buddhism, and Vedanta of Hinduism.

### Views of Buddhism

There are several different schools of thought within Buddhism and most of them believe that there is no permanent and unchanging Reality or substance underneath the phenomenal existence. This belief also means that human beings do not have any essence, or soul, either individually or collectively. This is a fundamental doctrine of Buddhism and known as the doctrine of *Anatman*, or No-Self. According to Buddhist philosophy everything in the phenomenal existence is a part of causal chains of *Karma*, which are formed by successive actions and reactions. What we see and experience is an ever-changing process of continuous Becoming, and there is no Being, or beings. An individual person is nothing but a collection of different aggregates, or *Skandhas*, which are constantly changing. These aggregates are: marterial form (*Rupa*), sensation (*Vedana*), perception (*Samjna*), disposition or mental formations (*Samskara*), and consciousness (*Vijnana*). All the aggregates are causally interconnected and constantly changing. Some schools of Buddhist philosophy believe that Reality is nothing but momentary existences whereas some believe that there is a continuously existing but continuously *changing* substance. As I mentioned earlier most schools agree that there is no unchanging substance in any of these aggregates. Further, there is no subject, or agent, behind a conscious act although there is an ego sense of a doer and experiencer. For example, when a thought arises there is no thinker distinct from it; it is the thought that thinks. So the concept of immortality and rebirth of souls in the traditional sense is not applicable to Buddhism.

That Buddhist philosophy does not believe in the concept of rebirth of souls surprises many common persons since in Buddhist literature there is considerable discussion about *Samsara* (the cycles of birth and rebirth), and one of the goals of Buddhist spiritual practice is for a 'soul' to get out of *Samsara* and attain Nirvana, which is a non-dual state of peace and silence. (There are different interpretations of what Nirvana is.) However, it is important to understand that for Buddhism the entity that is reborn is not a soul, i.e., a spiritual entity, but it represents the continuation of the chain of *Karma*. In Sri Aurobindo's words, "In the Buddhist theory rebirth is imperative because Karma compels it; not a soul, but Karma is the link of an apparently continuing consciousness, -- for the consciousness changes from moment to moment: there is this apparent continuity of consciousness, but there is no real immortal soul taking birth and passing through the death of the body to be reborn in another body." (The Life Divine, p. 747, footnote)

Views of Traditional Vedanta

Vedanta represents the philosophy of Upanishads, Brahma Sutras, and Bhagavad Gita (or Gita). (The Upanishads are the original source of Vedanta.) There are a few different schools of thought within this system of philosophy based on the interpretations of certain Indian theologians/philosophers. Adwaita (Non-Dual) Vedanta is one of these schools, and it was developed by Shankaracharya (Shankara). The other two prominent schools are Vishistha Adwaita (Qualified Non-Dualism) and Dwaita (Dualism), and these were developed by Ramanujacharya (Ramanuja) and Madhvacharya (Madhva) respectively. According to Shankara the reality of individual souls and their rebirth are merely a conventional (*byabaharik*) truth and these do not have any ultimate (*paramarthik*) truth because it is only the silent and inactive Brahman, the Supreme Reality, that is real and everything else is false and like a dream. As Sri Aurobindo explained, "The Self in this view is one, it cannot be many or multiply itself; there cannot be any true individual, only at most a one Self omnipresent and animating each mind and body with the idea of an 'I'." (The Life Divine, p. 752, Footnote) Shankara believed that there is an individual spiritual self (*Jivatman* or *Jiva*), but it exists only as long as one lives in ignorance. After many births and rebirths when ignorance is removed, *Jiva* realizes that it is not different from the universal Self (Atman) and it merges with it. Then it loses its individuality, and thereafter it is not reborn again.

Ramanuja believed that a *Jiva* is real and an eternal portion of Ishwara (God). He believed that an individual spiritual self in essence is identical with Self, but at the same time it is distinct from Self in some respects and it depends on God (Ishwara). The dualistic school of Madhva also treats an individual self to be eternal and real but constituted by its own unique substance. Thus for Madhva an individual self is different from God as well as from other individual selves. Madhva's philosophy is pluralistic. For Ramanuja and Madhva, an individual soul maintains its individuality even when its ignorance is removed and it gets out of the *Samsara*. The liberated souls remain with God in a blissful state of consciousness.

## Views of Sri Aurobindo

Traditional interpretation of Adwaita Vedanta does not present a meaningful purpose for the existence of an individual and his rebirth, and it is puzzling why an individual will come into phenomenal existence at all if getting out of this existence and *Samsara* should be his goal. However, all Upanishads do not present a negative view toward life on earth, and Isha Upanishad is a good example of those that embrace both Being and Becoming. Sri Aurobindo believed in the concept of Adwaita, or non-dualism, but he also believed in the reality and immortality of individual souls. He added to the views of Upanishads an evolutionary perspective, which gives human existence and rebirth a meaningful purpose. Sri Aurobindo pointed out that whereas the physical evolution of species has received the attention of scientists and scholars, what is overlooked is the evolution of consciousness, which is taking place simultaneously. Rebirth of souls is the necessary mechanism for this spiritual evolution.

In Sri Aurobindo's view, which fully agrees with the view of Upanishads, this universe is the self-creation of a supreme Reality, and Spirit is the substance of everything; all things are various powers and forms of the Spirit. *Sachchidananda*, which is an infinite existence, an infinite consciousness and force, and an infinite delight of being, hid itself in an apparent nescience, and now it is manifesting itself more and more through matter, life and mind. The emerging consciousness at the levels of matter and life had to take numerous forms, which include the forms of plants and animals, until it reached human level where mind has emerged. However, the evolution of consciousness has not stopped with the first appearance of mind, and it is continuing to reach higher levels. There is a large difference between the mind of an uneducated primitive man and that of a present-day educated man. Sri Aurobindo believed that the leading principle of mind at the present time, which is intellect, does not represent mind's highest stage, and that mental consciousness will reach even higher levels.

Thus according to Sri Aurobindo the real meaning of evolution is the gradual ascent of consciousness, and it is accompanied by the development of suitable bodies. Reaching the highest level of consciousness from the unconscious existence by a single leap is not the rule of its operation. By residing in Nature within each type of body individual souls grow by a variety of experience and are progressively enriched. Rebirth of individual souls is necessary for this progressive growth. In Sri Aurobindo's words, "It is through the conscious individual being that this recovery is possible; it is in him that the evolving consciousness becomes organized and capable of awaking to its own Reality. The immense importance of the individual being, which increases as he rises in the scale, is the most remarkable and significant fact of a universe which started without consciousness and without individuality in an undifferentiated Nescience. The importance can only be justified if the Self as individual is no less real than the Self as cosmic Being or Spirit and both are powers of the eternal." (The Life Divine, P. 755) Sri Aurobindo points out that it is only by taking birth in a physical body, which provides a separative form that a soul can develop through the play of relations between an individual and other individuals. Eventually this progressive development leads to the recovery of unity of a soul with other souls and with God.

In addition to his clear view about the role of individual souls in the evolution of consciousness, Sri Aurobindo presented a clear idea about what exactly he means by a human soul and what is it that is reborn. He explained that "The human birth in this world is on its spiritual side a complex of two elements, a spiritual Person and a soul of personality; the former is man's eternal being, the latter is his cosmic and mutable being. As the spiritual impersonal person he is one in his nature and being with the freedom of *Sachchidananda* who has here consented to or willed his involution in the Nescience for a certain round of soul-experience, impossible otherwise, and presides secretly over its evolution. As the soul of personality he is himself part of that long development of the soul-experience in the forms of Nature; ..." (The Life Divine, p. 759) The individual spiritual person is *Jivatman*, or *Jiva*, which remains outside the phenomenal Nature. *Jivatman* is unchanging and unborn, but it has its representative in Nature, which participates in the life of a person in the phenomenal world. This representative is the mutable purusha, or soul, supporting the outer personality, and Sri Aurobindo calls it 'psychic being', or *chaitya purusha*. It is the psychic being that is reborn, and it grows by the experience gained from life activities.

In traditional Hindu philosophy *Karma* is considered to be the primary factor that determines the need of rebirth as well the nature of the new life that is assumed by a soul after rebirth. There is another common belief that the soul returns to a new life with most of the outer personality of the present life intact. According to Sri Aurobindo these concepts are only partially true, and he emphasized that the factor that plays the most important role in the process of rebirth is the need of a soul, or psychic being, to grow and attain new experience, and according to him after death the psychic being of a person assimilates the experience of the past life and keeps only a small portion of the outer personality to bring to the new life. In his own words, "In each return to earth the Person, the Purusha, makes a new formation, builds a new personal quantum suitable for a new experience, for a new growth of its being. When it passes from its body, it keeps still the same vital and mental form for a time, but the forms or sheaths dissolve and what is kept is only the essential elements of the past quantum, of which some will but some may not be used in the next incarnation." (Life Divine, P. 817) Sri Aurobindo also said that in the case of an advanced spiritual person whose mental and vital personalities have undergone spiritual transformation in the present life, a large portion of the outer personality can be preserved. [For gaining a better understanding of these issues readers are encouraged to read a chapter of the Life Divine, which is titled 'Rebirth and Other Worlds; Karma, the Soul and Immortality'.]

It should be pointed out that the concept of psychic being and its evolution through the process of rebirth is not found in traditional Vedanta and it is a contribution of Sri Aurobindo to spiritual philosophy and yoga. With regard to an individual self traditional Vedanta usually refers to 'ego self' (*Ahamkara*), which is the lower self, and *Jivatman*, which is the higher self, whereas Sri Aurobindo's philosophy includes 'psychic being' along with 'ego self' and *Jivatman*. However, a few Upanishads refer to a soul in the spiritual heart, which is similar to psychic being. For example, Verse II. 3. 17 of Katha Upanishad says,

"The Purusha, the Spirit within, who is no larger than the finger of a man is seated always in the heart of creatures: one must separate Him with patience from one's own body as one separates from a blade of grass its main fibre. Thou shalt know Him for the Bright Immortal, yea, for the Bright Immortal."

Sri Aurobindo believed that the above verse is referring to psychic being. Readers may also consult Verse III. 14. 3 of Chandogya Upanishad, and Verse III. 13 of Svetasvatara Upanishad. According to Sri Aurobindo psychic being is the pure divine element in our consciousness. In his own words, "It is the concealed Witness and Control, the hidden Guide, the Daemon of Socrates, the inner light or inner voice of the mystic. It is that which endures and is imperishable in us from birth to birth, untouched by death, decay or corruption, an indestructible spark of the Divine." (The Life Divine, p. 225) Psychic being plays a very important role not only in Sri Aurobindo's philosophy but also in his integral yoga.

## Conclusions and Comments

There is a variety of beliefs about the immortality of souls and rebirth in both western and eastern cultures. In western philosophy belief in the immortality of souls is relatively more accepted than that in the rebirth of souls. Only a few ancient philosophers such as Pythagoras and Plato accepted the concept of the rebirth of souls. Many modern western philosophers reject the concepts of immortality as well as rebirth of souls, and most of them believe in materialism. However, there are also many modern philosophers who are not materialistic, and some of them accept the immortality of souls. In modern academic circle the common concepts of God, souls and rebirth are viewed as being too speculative. Most theologians of different western religions believe in souls and their immortality, but they do not believe in reincarnation. Only the mystical dimensions of western religions believe in the rebirth of souls. The definition of a soul in western culture is different among philosophers and theologians. At least so far as immortality is concerned, for most of the western philosophers, except Plato, it is the mind, or a higher aspect of mind, of a person that is considered to be his soul. For Plato and western theologians, however, soul tends to include mind and also the vital forces that animate a body.

Reincarnation or rebirth of souls is widely accepted in eastern religions. Rebirth is a fundamental tenet of Hinduism. Buddhism is unique as it believes in rebirth, but does not believe in souls. According to Buddhism it is the chain of Karma that causes certain formations of sensations and consciousness of a human being, which are called aggregates or *Skandhas,* to be reborn. In Indian philosophies, mind is considered to be a part of Nature and an instrument of soul. For Hindu philosophy a soul refers to consciousness, which remains hidden behind various parts of Nature including mind but it is intimately connected with Nature.

Sri Aurobindo acknowledges that human intellect cannot find satisfactory answers to questions about what we were before birth and what we will be after death. According to him we need to examine these questions in the context of the nature, source, and object of the cosmic movement. If we restrict ourselves to accepting only what can be proven by science or logical analysis using our intellect, we have to believe that our existence in this world as individual persons ends with the death of our bodies. In that case it will be hard to find any meaning and purpose for our existence, and we will have to agree with some of the twentieth century existential philosophers who hold that life in this world has no intrinsic value. Sri Aurobindo acknowledges that: "If there is no soul, then there can be a mechanical evolution without necessity or significance and birth is only part of this curious and senseless machinery. If the individual is only a temporary formation beginning and ending with the body, then evolution can be a play of the All-Soul or Cosmic Existence mounting through a progression of higher and higher species towards its own utmost possibility in this Becoming or to its highest conscious principle; rebirth does not exist and is not needed as a mechanism of that evolution". (The Life Divine, p. 764) However, for Sri Aurobindo and many other highly spiritual persons the existence of individual souls is not dependent on the body. According to them the process of rebirth is real and a necessary mechanism for the evolution of consciousness. Understanding the process of the evolution of consciousness is important for all human beings because we have reached a stage where instead of being passive participants we can actively and consciously participate in this process and thus help speed up the progress of spiritual evolution. According to Sri Aurobindo rebirth offers the firm assurance that imperfect individual beings will be able to attain perfection and eventually a divine life will be established on this earth.

## Brief Bibliography

Ariel, David S., *What Do Jews Believe?: The Spiritual Foundations of Judaism*", Schocken Books, New York, 1995

Abraham, Azriel, and Waxman, Bob, *Kabbaalah Simply Stated: A Conversation with the Rabbi*, Paragon House, 2004

Gethin, Rupert, *The Foundations of Buddhism*, Oxford University Press, 1998

Hick, John, *Philosophy of Religion*, Prentice-Hall, 1963

Rouse, W. H. D. (Translator), Great Dialogues of Plato, A Signet Classic, Penguin Putnam Inc., 1999

Sri Aurobindo, *The Problem of Rebirth*, Sri Aurobindo Ashram Trust, 1973

Sri Aurobindo, *The Life Divine*, Sri Aurobindo Ashram Trust, 1973

Sri Aurobindo, *The Upanishads*, Sri Aurobindo Ashram Trust, 1981

Wolfson, Harry A., "Immortality and Resurrection in the Philosophy of the Church Fathers", *Religious Philosophy: A Group of Essays*, Atheneum, New York, 1965 (Originally Published by Harvard University Press)

Wolfson, Harry A., *The Philosophy of Spinoza*, Volumes I and II, Schocken Books, New York, 1969

# Chapter 6

## Free Will and Determinism According to Vedanta and Western Philosophy

Free will and determinism are important issues in Eastern as well as Western philosophies and have been addressed by philosophers of all ages. These issues are debated by common persons too. In this article I cannot examine all aspects of these issues, and I will focus on the views of Vedanta philosophy and examine the issues from the perspective of an individual human being. I will also discuss the views of western religions and philosophers briefly.

In the context of our discussion determinism refers to the view that every event that has happened in the past, or is happening now, is a result of a prior event, and further that every event that occurs now will produce an effect in the future. Thus according to determinism every event is part of a causal chain and determined by a preceding cause. The causal laws of determinism may be physical and/or psychological (mental). Free will refers to our power to make a choice from alternative courses of actions which are available to us. We are considered to be using our free will when more than one course of action are available to us and we are able to take a certain action based on our own intention without any influence of causal laws. It should be noted that the word freedom also is used in the same sense of free will. However, freedom in some contexts refers to the environment or condition within which a person acts, and it covers a variety of situations — external as well as internal. Determinism and free will have implications for moral responsibility.

### HINDU VIEW

Hindu philosophy includes six different schools of thought, and these are Samkhya (of Kapila), Yoga (of Patanjali), Nyaya, Vaisheshika, Purva Mimamsa, and Vedanta. These schools do not hold exactly the same view with regard to certain aspects of determinism and freedom although all of them admit the concept of *karma*. As I mentioned earlier this article will focus on the views of Vedanta philosophy. Vedanta represents the most prominent Hindu philosophy. My primary sources of Vedanta philosophy for this article are Bhagavad Gita (or Gita) and a few relevant verses from the Upanishads. I will also present the views of two prominent Indian philosophers and scholars of Vedanta: Swami Vivekananda and Sri Aurobindo. First I will examine the widely known doctrine of *karma*, and then I will present the views of Vedanta.

### The Doctrine of *Karma*

The Sanskrit word *karma* can mean either action or the consequence of an action depending on the context it is used in. In Vedic literature *karma* means rituals. In the Upanishads *karma* is used in the sense of willed actions and also in the sense of the results of such actions. One of the earliest references to the doctrine of *karma* is in Verse 3. 2. 13 of Brihadaranyaka Upanishad, which says, "One indeed becomes good by good action, evil by evil action." In the same Upanishad the idea of karma is repeated in the Verse 4. 4. 5: "According as one acts, according as one behaves, so does one become. The doer of good becomes good, the doer of evil becomes evil."

The doctrine of *karma* is mentioned not only in Vedantic literature but also in the Puranas and the Itihasas, and there is a variety of ideas associated with this doctrine among common per sons. There are also some misconceptions regarding the concept of *karma*. For example, some persons associate *karma* with fate. According to the believers of fate the major events, if not all events, of one's life are predestined to happen. There is no universally agreed definition of what fate is and how rigidly it is applicable to a person's life; however, there is agreement that it is not the will of the supreme Divine. Commonly it is viewed as the will of a smaller or lesser god. There are other words used in the same sense and these include *niyati* and *adrista*, which also mean destiny or fate. To equate *karma* with fate is wrong.

According to the doctrine of *karma* every action has a consequence, which may or may not manifest immediately. There is a common notion that *karma* is a precise system of rewards and punishment based on the nature of our actions, but that is not true. Sri Aurobindo explained: "If we touch fire, it burns, but there is no principle of punishment in this relation of cause and effect, it is a lesson of relation and a lesson of experience; so in all Nature's dealings with us there is a relation of things and there is a corresponding lesson of experience." (LD, p. 814).

*Karma* is a cosmic law and is applicable to all grades of existence in the phenomenal world — physical world as well as supraphysical worlds of life force, emotions, and mind. The rigidity with which the law of *Karma* works depends on the grade of existence. At the physical level the law of *karma* is very deterministic and there is no room for freedom. On the other hand, at the mental level of human beings, where a higher level of consciousness operates, it seems that there is some room for free will, but that is what the debate is about. In any case, the doctrine of *karma* does not absolve its agent from moral responsibility for his actions. Although it fully recognizes the effects of past on the present, it does not completely deny us the possibility of choosing a particular course of action. This aspect of *karma* is explained by Dr. Radhakrishnan who wrote, "The cards in the game of life are given to us. We do not select them. They are traced to our past Karma, but we can call as we please, lead what suit we will, and as we play, we gain or lose. And there is freedom." (Radhakrishnan, p. 54) The same idea was conveyed by Swami Abhedananda who wrote, "A believer in the law of *karma* is a free agent and is responsible for all the good and bad results of his own actions that attend to his life. He knows that he creates his own destiny, and moulds his character by his thoughts and deeds." (Swami Abhedananda, pp. 14-15) It is important to note that the freedom that the law of *karma* offers is not granted to everyone automatically; the access to freedom requires one to act with a certain level of awareness, which all human beings do not have. Thus the doctrine of *karma* recognizes causality or determinism, and it also recognizes that causality does not take away free will completely. In other words, for *karma* determinism and free will are not mutually exclusive and they co-exist. This view is similar to the concept of compatibilism of western philosophy, which I will examine later.

Before moving on, I would like to mention that the doctrine of *karma* includes a variety of ideas many of which are related to life after death and also rebirth. It is a popular belief among Hindus that some of the consequences of a person's actions in the current life may be carried over to the next life. The doctrine of *karma* has many detailed aspects, and it recognizes that there are different types of *karma* such as *prarabhda, sanchita, kriyamana,* and *agami*. Definitions of these types of *karma* and explanation of how rigidly these are effective can be found in the general literature on the doctrine of *karma*. However, these ideas are not mentioned in the Upanishads or the Gita, and I will not discuss them in this article.

**Vedanta's Views**

Vedanta philosophy admits determinism in the form of the doctrine of *karma* according to which our actions bind us to a chain of causes and effects. Vedanta philosophy also admits the freedom of choice, or free will. To understand the apparently conflicting views one must delve into a fundamental metaphysical concept of Vedanta, which is brought out clearly in the Gita. The Gita's view on determinism and freedom is based on the concept of *Prakriti* (Nature) and *Purusha* (Soul, or Conscious Being). *Prakriti*, which makes up the phenomenal world, is subject to causal laws, while *Purusha* (in its higher status) is essentially free. Thus the Gita and the Upanishads make a distinction between the true Soul, or higher self, of an individual person and his apparent soul, or lower self. The higher Self transcends Nature, which constitutes the phenomenal world of time and space, and thus is free from its determinism. The apparent soul is *ahamkara*, the ego, and being constructed by Nature is subject to its control. Ordinarily, we identify ourselves with our ego and become enslaved to Nature and her modes or qualities, called *Gunas*. We are driven by desires, and our will and actions are entirely determined by the causal laws of Nature. In spite of that we generally feel and think that we are freely choosing our actions. In the words of the Gita, "All the actions are being entirely done by the modes (*gunas*) of Nature; the ego-deluded being regards his "I" as the doer". (Verse III. 27)

Vedanta philosophy recognizes three Gunas — *Sattva, Rajas,* and *Tamas. Sattva* is the mode of understanding, light, and purity; *Rajas* is the mode of passion and action; and *Tamas* represents the mode of darkness and inertia. These three modes bind us to the lower nature. In the Gita's words, "*Sattva, Rajas* and *Tamas* are *gunas* born of *Prakriti;* they bind to the body the imperishable Dweller in the body". (Verse XIV — 5) Although it is not difficult to see how *Tamas* and *Rajas* would limit our freedom, it may be difficult to see how *Sattva* also does the same. However, the Gita is quite clear on this issue and points out that *Sattva* too causes attachment to knowledge and happiness. The sense of ego does not disappear when a person acts in the mode of *Sattva.*

To free oneself from the determinism of Nature and its modes, one must clearly recognize the operation of the modes of Nature. Gita (XIII. 29) says, "He who sees that all actions are all ways done by Prakriti and also sees the Self as non-doer, he (truly) sees." Next, one has to rise to a higher plane of existence and find one's higher Self, which is free. The concepts of lower and higher selves are presented in the Upanishads as well. There are two verses in Mundaka Upanishad and also in Svetasvatara Upanishad, which use the metaphor of two birds to refer to the lower and higher selves of an individual person. The verses are as follows:

1. Two birds, closely united companions, cling to the very same tree. Of these two, one eats the sweet fruit (of the tree), (and) the other looks on without eating. (Mundaka III. 1, and Svetasvatara IV. 6)
2. On the same tree, a person (individual soul) immersed (in ignorance) and deluded, grieves on account of his helplessness. When he sees the other, the Lord who is worshipped and his greatness, he becomes freed from sorrow. (Mundaka III. 2, and Svetasvatara IV. 7)

These verses are describing two statuses of an individual soul (*purusha*). One of the birds represents the soul involved in *Prakriti*, which Gita refers to as the *kshara*, mutable. This *kshara* identifies itself with the ego and is bound up helplessly in the actions of the *Gunas* along with the laws of causality. Trapped in *Prakriti* this soul forgets its higher nature, which is represented by the other bird. This higher nature belongs to *Atman* (Self). (The other bird can be interpreted as *Jivatman,* the individual self, which is a centre of Atman, the universal Self.) *Atman* is beyond the control of *Prakriti,* and Gita refers to it as *akshara,* immutable. When ignorance is removed and a person's ego is replaced by the higher Self, one gains liberation from the determinism of *Prakriti* and the laws of causality.

I should add that the concept of *Prakriti* and *Purusha* is found in both Sankhya and Vedanta philosophies, but there is a significant difference in their views as to the relation between Nature and Soul. Whereas Sankhya philosophy is dualistic and treats *Prakriti* and *Purusha* as two separate principles, Vedanta considers *Prakriti* and *Purusha* as two aspects of one principle, which is *Brahman.* Vedanta's *Prakriti* (Nature) is the power inherent in *Purusha* and the driving force of the phenomenal world. According to Gita *Prakriti* (Nature) has higher and lower statuses. The higher Nature is the supreme nature (*Para-Prakriti*) of God, and it is the conscious power of God. The ignorant power or force operating in the phenomenal world is the lower *Prakriti* (*Apara-Prakriti*). In the manifested phenomenal world *Purusha* loses itself in the mutable lower *Prakriti* and it seems to change with the changes of Nature. Gita refers to the *Purusha* hidden in the lower *Prakriti* as *kshara Purusha* (mutable soul). *Purusha* in its aspect of pure Being, which transcends the lower *Prakriti,* is *akshara Purusha* (unchanging soul), also called *Atman.*

There is another important difference between Sankhya and Vedanta as presented in the Gita with regard to the relation of *Purusha* with *Prakriti.* Sankhya's *Purusha* passively witnesses and sustains the actions of Prakriti, but it does not govern her actions. According to Sankhya when *Purusha* withdraws its sanction *Prakriti*'s actions come to an end. According to the Gita (XIII. 22) *Purusha* is more than just a witness and consenter; it can also be Ishwara, the Lord and controller of Nature.

The Gita does not advocate that one should completely withdraw from action and remain merged in blissful inaction with *akshara Purusha*, the inactive silent Self (*Atman*). One indeed can become free from the determinism of Nature by realizing Self (*Atman*); that is the path followed by "the Sannyasin, who rejects the nature, the action altogether, so far at least as action can be rejected, so that there may be an unmixed undivided freedom; but that solution, though admitted, is not preferred by the Gita". (Sri Aurobindo, EG, p. 222) According to the Gita the first stage is to be united with the Self and remain unaffected by desire and passion, success and failure; but one must not stop there. Sri Krishna urges Arjuna to fight. The Gita wants us to be active in our life. The *Isha Upanishad* also recommends action. Verse 2 of *Isha Upanishad* says, "Doing verily works in this world one should wish to live a hundred years. There is no other way for you but this. This way action does not stick to a man." But how can one act in the world and still remain free from determinism? To understand the Gita's answer to this question we must understand the concepts of *kshara Purusha*, *akshara Purusha*, and Purushottama, and the higher *Prakriti* or *Para-Prakriti*.

Some interpreters of Vedanta view the statuses of *kshara* and *akshara* Purushas as being the only two alternatives, which for them are mutually exclusive. The Gita does not accept that view and recognizes a third status, which is "a supreme reality of the Soul's existence of which these are two contrary aspects, but which is limited by neither of them". (Sri Aurobindo, EG, p. 220) This supreme reality is the Gita's Purushottama. This concept is clearly stated in the verses 16 and 17 of Chapter XV, which say: "There are two *Purushas* in this world, the immutable (*akshara*) and the mutable (*kshara*); the mutable is all these existences, the high-seated consciousness (*kutastha*) is called the immutable (*akshara*). But other than these two is the highest spirit called the supreme Self (Purushottama), who enters the three worlds and upholds them, the imperishable Lord (Ishvara)."

The Gita recognizes that to be free from the chain of causality one must attain the status of *akshara* Purusha and thus become *trigunatita*, superior to the three *gunas*; but *akshara* Purusha, the *Atman*, is silent and inactive — *akarta,* non-doer. Therefore, by reaching *akshara* Purusha one can liberate oneself from Nature's determinism, but there one cannot find the divine Will for work. To find the divine Will one must go beyond *akshara* Purusha and unite his whole being with Purushottama and *Para-Prakriti*, which is the supreme nature and executive force of Purushottama. The Gita refers to it in Verses 4 and 5 of Chapter 7: "The five elements, mind, reason, and ego, comprise my eightfold divided Nature. This is the lower. But know my other Nature different from this, the supreme, which becomes the *Jiva* (individual self) and by which the world is upheld."

When one is able to unite one's whole being with Purushottama, one can find poise in *akshara Purusha* and be free from the control of *Prakriti*, and at the same time one can carry out one's work in the world as an instrument of the divine Will, which is in *Para-Prakriti*. *Purusha* can change the motive of *Prakriti*'s action and make it perform selfless and desireless actions by unifying it with the divine Will. Such work does not bind one to the causal chain.

To become egoless and unite with one's higher Self one must go beyond the determinism of Nature; but this is not an easy task. However, the Gita presents a practical way for this purpose, which is the triple path of knowledge, works and devotion. According to the Gita we must sincerely feel that the fruits of our actions belong not to us but to the Master of the world, Purushottama, and we must consecrate to Him all our actions, thoughts and feelings. We must see God everywhere and in everything and also see everything residing in God. Thus, gradually we can feel oneness with all beings and lose our egoistic self and selfish desires. Finally, we must lovingly make a complete surrender to Purushottama and His Will.

There are several verses in the Gita that describe how one should act in order not to accumulate adverse *karma*. Among these, the following two verses perhaps are the most revealing: "Whatever you do, whatever you eat, whatever you offer (in sacrifice), whatever you give, whatever spiritual austerities you perform, make it an offering to Me. Thus, you will be liberated from good and evil results, which constitute the bonds of action; with thy soul in union with the Divine through renunciation, you shall be free and attain to Me". (Verses IX — 27 and 28.)

**The Views of Two Great Scholars of Vedanta: Swami Vivekananda and Sri Aurobindo**

The views of Swami Vivekananda and Sri Aurobindo on free will and determinism are very similar to those of the Gita. Both of them recognize the determinism of Nature manifested in the phenomenal world of time and space. Swami Vivekananda used a forceful language to make the point that there is no free will or freedom from causality, as long as we live an ordinary life dominated by Nature. Referring to *karma*, or the law of causation, he said, "It is only when 'being' or existence gets moulded into name and form that it obeys the law of causation, and is said to be under law; because all law has its essence in causation. Therefore, we see at once that there cannot be any such thing as free will; the very words are a contradiction, because will is what we know, and everything that we know is within our universe, and everything within our universe is moulded by the conditions of space, time, form, and causation." (CW, Volume. I, p. 95 — 96) It is very important that we do not overlook the context in which this and similar statements were made by Swami Vivekananda since that may give the idea that he did not believe in freedom under any circumstances. In fact, he made other statements in equally forceful language emphasizing the ability of human beings to rise above the limits of Nature and attain freedom from causality. For example, he also said, "The Vedanta says that Infinity is our true nature; it will never vanish, it will abide forever. But we are limiting ourselves by our Karma, which like a chain round our necks has dragged us into this limitation. Break that chain and be free. Trample law under your feet. There is no law in human nature, there is no destiny, no fate." (CW, Volume II, p. 323) He pointed out that weakness of human nature is what leads us to the belief in fate, and he said, "We human beings are very slow to recognize our own weakness, our own faults, so long as we can lay the blame upon somebody else. Men in general lay all blame of life on their fellow-men, or, failing that, on God, or they conjure up a ghost, and say it is fate. What is fate, and who is fate? We reap what we sow. We are the makers of our own fate." (CW, Volume II, p. 224) Swami Vivekananda makes a clear distinction between our phenomenal nature, which is determined by *Prakriti* and its *gunas*, and our true Self, which is not bound by nature. His message is that we must find our true Self and become free even while living our life on earth under any circumstances.

Sri Aurobindo repeatedly points out that free-will and determinism are not mutually exclusive, which means that one does not preclude the other. He commented, "All is free-will or all is destiny — it is not so simple as that". (LY, Part One, p. 467) He also pointed out, "A certain absolute freedom is one aspect the soul's relation with Nature at one pole of our complex being; a certain absolute determinism by Nature is the opposite aspect at its opposite pole; and there is also a partial and apparent, therefore an unreal eidolon of liberty which the soul receives by a contorted reflection of these two opposite truths in the developing mentality". (EG, p. 203)

Sri Aurobindo's philosophy recognizes a gradation of consciousness that exists among various types of beings in the world beginning with material objects and moving up to plants, animals and human beings. He believes that the level of determinism varies according to the grade of consciousness. He wrote, "For practical purposes, on the surface there is an entire determinism in matter — though this is now disputed by the latest school of Science. As Life emerges a certain plasticity sets in, so that it is difficult to predict anything exactly as one predicts material things that obey a rigid law. The plasticity increases with the growth of Mind, so that man can have at least a sense of free-will, of a choice of his action, of a self-movement which at least helps determine circumstances. But this freedom is dubious because it can be declared to be an illusion, a device of Nature, part of its machinery of determination, only a seeming freedom or at most a restricted, relative and subject independence. It is only when one goes behind away from *Prakriti* to *Purusha* and upward away from Mind to spiritual Self that the side of freedom comes to be first evident and then, by unison with the Will which is above Nature, complete." (LY, Part 1, p. 474 — 475) According to Sri Aurobindo "action does not bind or limit our true being at all. Action has no such effect on the spiritual

Person or *Purusha* or on the psychic entity within us, it binds or limits only the surface constructed personality." (LD, p. 460)

Sri Aurobindo believed strongly in divine grace and he wrote, "Destiny in the rigid sense applies only to the outer being so long as it lives in the Ignorance.... But as soon as one enters the path of spiritual life, this old predetermined destiny begins to recede. There comes in a new factor, the divine Grace, the help of a higher Divine Force other than the force of *Karma*, which can lift the *sadhak* (a spiritual practitioner) beyond the present possibilities of his nature. One's spiritual destiny is then the divine election which ensures the future." (LY, p. 475)

The same view on *karma* and grace is expressed by Sri Ramakrishna, the spiritual teacher of Swami Vivekananda, through the example of a cow tied to a post by a rope. The cow's freedom of movement is limited to the circle of space determined by the length of the rope. Similarly an ordinary person is bound by his *karma*, which limits his freedom like the rope in the case of the cow. Sri Ramakrishna also added to this example that when a person turns to God and spiritual practice, the length of the rope of *karma* increases; in other words, one's freedom increases in proportion to one's spiritual progress and the action of divine grace. (see SS, p. 108)

**WESTERN VIEW**

The issue of free will and determinism is a major topic of western theology and philosophy, and a separate article is needed to present a comprehensive review of the thoughts of western theologian and philosophers. However, instead of omitting any discussion of western views completely, I will present a brief discussion of the views that are generally recognized in western philosophy and theology. I also will present the views of a few major philosophers of the west. I should point out that there is another word that is used in the context of determinism and that word is 'destiny'. The word destiny often is used in the same sense as fate. However, a distinction also can be made between these two terms. In one sense fate can be regarded as a power (usually regarded as some sort of blindly operating force) that on some level determines the events or the outcomes in one's life, and these events or outcomes can be regarded as the destiny of that individual.

In addition to believing in fate, which we discussed earlier, many persons in the west believe in 'predestination', and there is a difference between these two concepts. Fate and fatalism refer to the action of some kind of "blind' force, whereas predestination involves God's will. God's omniscience is an important concept of Christianity, and many Christians believe that the future actions of people are known by God and thus our future actions are predetermined. Some Christians also believe that salvation after death can be achieved only by God's Grace and that God has predetermined who will receive His Grace and achieve salvation without considering what they actually do in their lives. The belief in some form of predestination is found in all major western religions — Christianity, Judaism and Islam. The concept of predestination raises a few questions. One famous theologian of the past who raised questions with regard to predestination is St. Augustine. The question that bothered him is: why should men be morally responsible for their actions if God knows what they will do ahead of their actions and if their salvation after death is also predetermined? Despite his misgivings about predestination St. Augustine argued that although God has foreknowledge of our actions, we have free-will and are morally responsible for our actions. His arguments are complicated and beyond the scope of the article.

Western views in modern times have been influenced by science and its discoveries. Many educated persons today believe in the universal laws of science and scientific determinism. Modern science is regarded by many people as covering not only physical events but also psychological events. It is also believed that even though the cause of an event is not known at the present time it could be found by continued research. There is also a concept that every event is a part of a causal chain and that there is a preceding or antecedent event (or events) that caused it, and that the current event will be followed by another of which it will be the cause. This concept is called determinism.

Fatalism, predestination, and determinism appear to be similar as according to these concepts the actions of a person and events are determined by some cause other than the agent, or person, who acts. However, there is a difference among these as to the underlying reason or cause that determines the events. In the case of fatalism and predestination the causes that determine major events is fate, which is a force of some type, and God's will respectively; thus the actions are unavoidable and have nothing to do with the agent of actions. Determinism usually deals with scientific or natural causes of events.

With regard to human behavior there are a few variations of determinism based on the extent that an act can be based on free will. These variations are called hard determinism, compatibilism, and libertarianism. To understand the differences among these variations we must distinguish between two types of freedom, or free will — circumstantial and metaphysical. The lack of circumstantial freedom is caused by obstacles such as physical disability, financial constraints, and coercion, which limit the options or choices available to a person. Metaphysical freedom is related to a person's ability to choose freely from the choices that are available to him. According to hard determinism free will and determinism are incompatible and we do not have free will; so our actions are pre-determined and we are not morally responsible for our actions. Compatibilism believes that determinism and free will can co-exist. It acknowledges that all events and human actions have causes, and that certain options may not be available due to circumstantial constraints or obstacles. It also believes that metaphysical freedom exists, and given all the constraints and influences we can choose to act in a certain way and so we are responsible for our actions. (This view is also called soft determinism.) Libertarianism is the opposite of hard determinism and it argues that free will is incompatible with determinism and that we have free will. According to libertarianism our actions are never wholly determined by antecedent events, and so we are morally responsible for our actions. (Philosophical or metaphysical libertarianism should not be confused with political libertarianism.) It may not be unfair to say that compatibilism is the most widely accepted concept among western philosophers.

Before I close this discussion about western views I will present very briefly the views of two famous philosophers — Baruch Spinoza (1632 — 1677) and Jean-Paul Sartre (1905 — 1980). Spinoza's philosophy is very different from the theological and philosophical views of the west both prevailing during his time and to this day. Judaism, Christianity, and Islam believe that God is different from the world. He creates the world and stands apart from it, even if He is not totally aloof from His creation. God is a person and has a will. He has a reciprocal relationship with human beings. Spinoza denied all these traditional concepts. His God is an impersonal principle or substance and the world is this very substance expressing its own internal dynamism. He believed that God is the only free cause in the sense that God alone acts from the laws of His own nature and is compelled by no one and by no other force. He also believed that, although God is 'free' in this sense, God does not have free will and any purpose for manifesting the world. God acts by the necessity of His own nature and is incapable of changing the course of His actions, and this means that whatever exists is how it must be. Human beings also do not have any free will and their acts in the world are causally related and determined by God's nature. With regard to the awareness or feeling of freedom in making choices, which human beings usually have, Spinoza's view is that it represents delusion and ignorance of true causes. However, he also speaks of a kind of "freedom," even if it does not come from free will, which can be possessed by human beings to the extent that they come to have insight regarding the true cause of everything.

Jean-Paul Sartre is a very famous philosopher of the twentieth century. He is considered by many to be the father of Existentialism, which is a recognized branch of philosophy. His views on free will and determinism are very different from those of Spinoza. Sartre was an atheist and did not believe in determinism. He believed that as conscious beings people have the freedom to choose from alternative courses of action, and he also believed that people are responsible for the actions they choose to perform. Although the exact interpretation is a matter for discussion, Sartre held, even more strongly, that in some sense human beings are themselves temporally extended acts of freedom. In other words, he believed in a total freedom that entails a total responsibility. According to him even those who choose not to act in a situation are still making a conscious choice for their inaction and thus are responsible for the consequences of their inaction. However, Sartre also prefers to reserve such terms as 'choice' and 'decision' for acts of freedom as they occur on a level of reflective consciousness.

Sartre talks about authenticity and believed that an action is authentic if it is chosen to be made with a clear awareness of the responsibility for that action. He, however, did not accept choices for actions that oppress or exploit others as authentic. Another phenomenon related to free will or freedom that Sartre discussed in his writings is that of anguish. He believed that freedom is hard to handle and most persons who realize that they must make their own choices for which they themselves will be responsible are terrified and suffer from anguish. But he also held that, even when anguish is not psychologically explicit, it is nonetheless a permanent part of the human condition.

## CONCLUDING REMARKS

In this article I examined the subject of free will and determinism from the perspectives of eastern and western cultures. There are similarities between these perspectives, and there are some differences too. A major difference between the views of western and eastern cultures is that both Hindus and Buddhists believe in the rebirth of a soul, and they also believe that the results of one's actions in the present life can be carried over to the next life. The rebirth of a soul is not commonly believed in the west. In this article I have not dealt with the issue of how *karma* and determinism may affect one's life after death and the rebirth of one's soul.

There are several different philosophies in the east, and I examined only the philosophy of Vedanta, which is the most prominent school of Hindu philosophy. The Vedanta philosophy recognizes that both determinism and free will are applicable to human beings, and that how bound or how free we are depends on our spiritual awareness. If we are not conscious of our spiritual self and do not know how to stand apart from the movements of our nature, we will be driven to action by desires and emotions and we will be overpowered by joy and grief, the consequences of successes and failures in actions. On the other hand if we are aware of the movements of nature — desires and emotions — within ourselves and can stand apart from them, we will be able to have control over nature and exercise free will. According to Vedanta the ideal way to attain freedom is to offer every action to God and leave the results in God's hand. In the Gita's words, "Having abandoned attachment, he who acts by dedicating his actions to Brahman is not stained by sin, even as water does not cling to a lotus leaf". (Verse V — 10)

Free will and determinism along with moral responsibility for actions are major topics in western philosophy and theology. Among the western philosophers some lean toward hard determinism, which denies free will, and some believe in libertarianism, which denies determinism. There are also those who believe in compatibilism according to which determinism and free will can coexist. I may point out that there are similarities between the concept of compatibilism of western philosophy and the views of Vedanta philosophy of India although there are differences too.

Among modern western philosophers the existentialists believe in a free will and that it is incompatible with determinism. They emphasize making conscious choices along with taking responsibility. Although there are major differences between existentialism and the philosophy of Vedanta, both philosophies emphasize the importance of consciousness with reference to free will. Sartre believed that a person's ability to make choices based on his free will depends on how reflectively conscious he is in his daily life. A similar concept is found in Vedanta philosophy as according to it a person needs to realize his inner self or soul (*purusha*) in order to be free from the determinism of *Prakriti* (Nature). The inner soul is experienced initially as a witness consciousness at the mental level, and it is similar to the reflective consciousness of Sartre. However, Sartre goes further and holds that it is of the very nature of human consciousness that a person is acting freely even when the acts of freedom that constitute his being do not occur on the level of reflective consciousness.

## References

Radhakrishnan, S., *The Hindu View of Life*, The Macmillan Company, 1971

Sartre, Jean-Paul, *Being and Nothingness*, Translated by Hazel E. Barnes, Washington Square Press, 1992

Solomon, Robert C., *The Little Philosophy Book*, Oxford University Press, 2008

Sri Aurobindo, *Letters on Yoga, Part One*, Sri Aurobindo Ashram Trust, 1971 [Abbreviated as LY]

Sri Aurobindo, *The Essays on the Gita*, Sri Aurobindo Ashram Trust, 1972 [Abbreviated as EG]

Sri Aurobindo, *The Life Divine*, Sri Aurobindo Ashram Trust, 1973 [Abbreviated as LD]

Sri Aurobindo, *Isha Upanishad*, Sri Aurobindo Ashram Trust, 2006

Swami Abhedananda, *Doctrine of Karma: A Study in Its Philosophy and Practice*, Ramakrishna Vedanta Math, Kolkata, India, Ninth Edition February 2008

Swami Saradananda, *Sri Ramakrishna the Great Master*, translated Swami Jagadananda (Chennai: Ramakrishna Math, 2010 [Abbreviated as SS]

Swami Vivekananda, *Collected Works, Volumes I and II*, Advaita Ashram, Calcutta 700-014, 1991 [Abbreviated as CW]

Wolfson, Harry A., *The Philosophy of Spinoza*, Volumes I and II, Schocken Books, 1969

# Chapter 7

## Jewish Mysticism and Hinduism: A Comparison

### Introduction

Every major religion of the world includes two types of understanding or view about the nature of God, His relation with the world and the way of approaching Him. The differences between these views seem to divide the theology of a religion into two groups or schools, viz., traditional and mystical. Many of the differences between the religions usually lie in metaphysical concepts and also the practices of respective religions. The practices deal mostly with rituals and observances. The mystical parts or aspects of different religions on the other hand have significant similarities. There are several Christian mystics whose views based on their personal mystical experiences are different from traditional Christian views in some respects and are similar to those of the mystics of Hinduism. For example, Meister Eckhart (1260 — 1328), a medieval Christian mystic, expressed his view of the oneness or unity of all beings. St. Teresa of Avila (1515 — 1582) also is known to have had mystical experiences. It may be noted that there are influences of the neo-Platonic ancient philosopher Plotinus on Eckhart. Plotinus' philosophy has a mystical element. Among modern western philosophers there are a few who recognized that there may be realms of consciousness beyond human intellect. Some philosophy scholars believe that there is a mystical element in the philosophy of the German philosopher Martin Heidegger with respect to his concept of 'Being' and how to experience it. A more contemporary example is Pierre Teilhard de Chardin (1881 — 1955), a Roman Catholic priest and philosopher, who saw divinity embedded in all objects of the world — animate and inanimate. The similarities of his views about spiritual evolution and universal consciousness and those of the Hindu philosopher Sri Aurobindo are recognized and discussed in several books and articles (Sethna, Zaehner). It is also well known that some of the views and practices of the Islamic mystical group Sufis have similarities with Hindu Yoga. For example, one of the goals of Sufi practitioners is to abandon all notions of dualism, or multiplicity, including the conception of an individual self, and to realize the Divine Unity. Rumi, whose full name was Jalal al-Din Rumi, is a famous mystical Sufi poet. The Jewish mystical tradition and Hinduism also have similarities, which are not well known, and this chapter will explore these similarities. This chapter will focus primarily on one subject or issue of theology — the concept of God and His relation with the world and its creatures. For Jewish mysticism I will draw mostly from the concepts of Kabbalah, and for Hinduism my main sources will be Vedanta philosophy of Bhagavad Gita (or simply Gita) and the writings of Sri Aurobindo, a scholar of Vedanta.

I would like to add that although I did not include a chapter in this book about Christian mysticism, its importance should not be overlooked. There are many good sources of information on Christian mysticism, and one good source to start with is the article by Gellman, which can be found on the Internet. (See References for more details.)

## Concepts of God in Traditional Judaism

The original source of traditional/orthodox Judaism is Torah, which includes the five books Moses — Genesis, Exodus, Leviticus, Numbers and Deuteronomy. Torah's five books and two more books, viz., Neviim and Ketuvim, together is known as Tanakh or Hebrew Bible. The teachings of these books were interpreted and taught by rabbis, who are ordained Jewish teachers, and tannaim, who are Jewish scholars. The theology of traditional Judaism is reflected in the teachings of rabbis and tannaim, and these teachings are recorded in the literature known as Mishnah. And then, together with further commentaries by rabbis and scholars on the Mishnah, the whole thing is called the Talmud. Rabbinic theology took different tones as it developed in various places of the world during different time periods as Jews dispersed in different countries in the Middle East and Europe.

There are two competing ideas about God, which are reflected in rabbinic theology. According to one view God is a transcendent Supreme Being who created the world, but remains outside of it. This concept emphasizes that God is unknowable and beyond the imagination of human beings. Further, God is impersonal and has no emotions. The difficulty for common people with the inaccessible character or status of God is obvious, and rabbinic theology overcame this difficulty by including a parallel idea that despite His transcendence God is personal and accessible to His creatures. He has emotions and hears man's prayers. These two different ideas about God — His transcendence and nearness — coexist in traditional Judaism. I should point out that the nearness of God does not imply His immanence in the world, or in other words there is still a separation between God and the world.

During the Middle Ages and later there were several Jewish philosophers who contributed to or commented upon Jewish theology. Some of them differed in various ways from the view of God as portrayed by traditional Judaism. Noteworthy among them are two famous philosophers, — Moses Maimonides (1135 - 1204) and Baruch Spinoza (1632 — 1677). While Maimonides believed only in the transcendence of God, Spinoza believed in His immanence as well as in a certain sort of transcendence. According to Maimonides the transcendent God has nothing in common with humanity; He is impersonal and inaccessible to men. No human properties can be ascribed to God. Maimonides in effect solved the paradox of transcendence versus immanence by choosing the former and rejecting the latter. Now, with regard to the creation of the world there has been considerable debate on what Maimonides believed, whether he accepted creation ex nihilo (out of nothing), or creation from a preexisting material substrate, or Aristotle's concept of the world as an eternal entity. There is some agreement among scholars that he believed in creation ex nihilo.

Spinoza's philosophy was very different from traditional views of Judaism and other western religions. The most startling difference is that he defined God as 'substance' and declared that everything composing the world is an expression, a kind of "emanation", from the essence, or 'Attributes', of this single substance. He also said that God has no personality and does not rule over the universe by providence. Because his views about God and the world were so different Spinoza was excommunicated by the rabbis of Amsterdam. It also should be mentioned that some aspects of Spinoza's views have arguably been misinterpreted by some scholars. There is a view that according to Spinoza God is identical with Nature and no more. However, a case can be made that this is not a correct interpretation and that Spinoza recognized both the immanence and the transcendence of God. I have presented a detailed discussion of this issue in another chapter (of this book), which focuses on Spinoza and Vedanta.

Maimonides did not reconcile the differences between the transcendent and immanent aspects of God and also those between the personal and impersonal aspects. Spinoza accepted both immanence and transcendence but did not reconcile the personal and impersonal aspects of God, giving up the former. It is the mystical traditions of Judaism that tried to reconcile all these different aspects of God. In the following sections of this chapter I will examine the concepts and views of mysticism in general and those of Kabbalah focusing on various aspects of God. I will also compare these views with those of Hinduism. Hinduism includes different schools of thought, and I will refer to the concepts of Hindu Vedanta philosophy and its interpretation by Sri Aurobindo.

## Nature of Mysticism

Laypersons commonly think of mysticism as concepts and practices that are esoteric and magical in nature. The interpretation of the possible hidden meanings of common rituals and practices of religions may also take the form of what can be called mystical interpretation. For this chapter, however, I will not deal with these aspects of mysticism, and I will focus only on theological (metaphysical) concepts dealing with God and His relation with the world. Before examining these metaphysical concepts in Jewish mysticism a few statements should be made about the general nature of mystical theology.

A common criticism of mysticism is that the theological concepts/views presented by mystics are based on neither rational arguments, nor empirical evidence, and so these concepts are considered by others as entirely speculative. To mystics, however, their views are based on personal experiences and intuitive knowledge, and to them their experiences are real. A mystic relies on introspection and delves into his deeper consciousness to find answers to questions about reality and truth. Mystics of all religions are known to practice contemplation and meditation, and they strive to go beyond the limits of intellect and intellectual logic. This personal or private aspect of mystical concepts is a source of criticism because these concepts and experiences cannot be verified by other persons unless they go through the same spiritual practices as the mystics do.

One important aspect of mysticism in general, which is different from traditional religious views, is the view of the 'interconnectedness' and 'oneness' of all that exists. This concept is generally related to the immanence of God in the world and its inhabitants, and according to this view everything in the world is a part of and united in the universal consciousness of God, who has become this world. Such a mystic sees God in everything and everything in God. These views of the immanence of God and the oneness of all are reflected in the Jewish mystical tradition of Kabbalah, and we will examine these in the following sections, but before I examine Kabbalah I would like to add another characteristic of mysticism.

Mysticism recognizes that the current state of human consciousness is not indicative of its full potential and true nature. Mysticism also believes that man not only is created in God's image but also is constituted of the same nature or substance. According to mystics the true divine nature is hidden and covered up by our relative ignorance, but it is possible to remove the cover of ignorance by spiritual aspiration and practices. The goal of a mystic is thus not only to come near to God but also to unite with divine consciousness. However, the experience of mystics with regard to the exact nature of this union with God varies. This union can be in the form of a total merger of individual consciousness with the divine with the loss of individuality, or a union while keeping a separation. The latter type of union with a separation is called 'cleaving', or 'devekut', in Judaism. In Jewish mysticism cleaving to God is the highest goal. As Gilya Schmidt (1995) explains in an article, the nature and status of devekut have changed from period to period and from location to location; however, there is no question that the attachment or adherence to God, which is implied by devekut, is more than traditional piety. In Hinduism also there are different paths for finding and uniting with God. One of those is the path of love and devotion (bhakti). A follower of the path of love and devotion strives for a loving and close relation of his soul with God while maintaining a separation. Constant remembrance of God is a recommended practice in Jewish mystical paths as well as in Hindu path of love and devotion.

### Origins of Jewish Mysticism and Kabbalah

The traditional Jewish concept of God is similar to the traditional views of other western religions. The point to note is that according to this view despite the nearness of God there is a real separation between man and God. Man can come close to God through prayer and other spiritual practices, but he cannot become one with Him. Furthermore, although traditional Judaism believes that God created man in His own image and that man can purify himself from many flaws of human nature, he cannot transform his own consciousness to become truly divine.

Jewish mysticism developed in different places in different times. The famous scholar of Jewish mysticism Grershom Scholem identified several periods of mystical movements within Judaism beginning with Merkabah mysticism in the first century AD. Other mystical traditions include Kabbalah, and Hasidism. Our focus will be primarily on Kabbalah, which is perhaps the most well-known and popular mystical movement of Judaism in modern times.

Kabbalah does not represent the totality of Jewish mysticism, of which it is only one phase. It first developed in the thirteenth century in Southern France and Spain and subsequently went through several phases of development in different locations. Perhaps the earliest text of Kabbalah is the book named Sefer ha-Bahir (Book of Bahir) written in late 1100s. An earlier book known as Sefer Yetzirah (Book of Creation) also contains ideas found in Kabbalah; however, this book is linked with the Merkabah mysticism, which preceded Kabbalah. The most influential text for Kabbalah is Sefer ha-Zohar (Book of Zohar). The Book of Zohar appeared first in Spain in late 1200s. It was published by Rabbi Moses de Leon, but it was based on an earlier text from the second century CE, which was written by rabbi Shimon bar Yochai also known as Rashbi. There are several other famous Kabbalists who then developed their own concepts within the framework of Kabbalah. Famous among them are Moses Cordovero and Isaac Luria, both of the sixteenth century. A detailed study of these different sources of thought within Kabbalah is beyond the scope of this chapter. However, there are a few concepts that are generally accepted by all schools within Kabbalah, and we will examine a few of these pertaining to the concept of God and His relation with the world, and how Kabbalah reconciles His transcendence and immanence.

**Eyn Sof and Sefirot of Kabbalah**

As I discussed earlier, Maimonides took the concept of God to one extreme by presenting the aspect of transcendence only. Spinoza recognized both immanence and transcendence, but his philosophy focused more on the immanent aspect. Kabbalists treated transcendence and immanence with equal emphasis, and they bridged the gap between them by introducing the concepts of Eyn Sof and Sefirot. (Eyn Sof may be spelled also as Ein Sof, or Ain Soph.) I will discuss these concepts in this section and present similar concepts found in Hinduism in the next section.

Kabbalists called the transcendent aspect of God as Eyn Sof, which means the Infinite, or without end. Eyn Sof belongs to the world of the infinite, and is unchanging and unknowable. Kabbalah recognizes that this transcendent aspect of God is impersonal and immutable, and it is not the proper object of prayers. Eyn Sof manifests or emanates the knowable world and at the same time maintains its transcendent status. In its emanated status, however, it is the essence of the manifested world and thus in that sense is immanent in it. According to the famous Kabbalist Moses Cordovero, "All existence is God: The essence of The Infinite is found in everything" (Matt, p. 24). Moses Cordovero also said, "God is everything that exists, though everything that exists is not God (Matt, p. 24).

It is interesting to note that the term Eyn Sof has a negative connotation implying 'no beginning' or 'non-being'. However, this concept of non-being is not nihilistic. The negative sense of the term indicates that the transcendent Godhead is indeterminable, and it is beyond any descriptions and concepts that can be presented by human language. It perhaps is more appropriate to describe Eyn Sof in terms of what it is not instead of what it is.

The concept of emanation helps Kabbalah describe the transition of Eyn Sof to the manifested world and thus bridge the gap between the transcendent and immanent aspects of God. According to Kabbalah the world is manifested via ten emanations from God, which continue to sustain the universe. Each of these emanations individually is called a Sefira, and all these ten Sefiras together are called Sefirot. (The term Sefirot is plural and the term Sefira is singular.) The ten individual Sefiras are organized in a specific hierarchy, and this hierarchical group is referred to as the Tree of Life. The emanations represent various qualities or powers, and before emanation occurs these qualities/powers are utterly united with and concealed within Eyn Sof. The Infinite Eyn Sof causes the Sefirot to emanate, and they in turn cause other stages of manifestation to occur. It should be pointed out that the realm of Sefirot lies above the manifested world and these powers act as the mediator between Eyn Sof and the manifested world.

The doctrine of Sefirot and the concept of Tree of Life are at the heart of Kabbalah. The role of each Sefira in the divine manifestation and the relation between these ten individual Sefiras themselves have been discussed by Kabbalah scholars in great detail; however, such an in-depth discussion is beyond the scope of this chapter. It also should be noted that there are different interpretations of the Tree of Life and how it is related to the manifested world. So the explanation that I will present may not match exactly with that of another interpreter. For our purpose it is important to recognize a few major ideas associated with Sefirot. The first Sefira, which stands at the head of the hierarchy, is called Keter, which means Crown. This is the first connection of the emanations with Eyn Sof. Some Kabbalists consider Keter as the 'Primal Will' or 'Divine Thought'. This may be considered the Godhead of manifestation. The next eight Sefiras and what they represent are as follows: Hokhmah (Wisdom), Binah (Understanding), Hesed (Mercy/Kindness), Gevurah (Strength/Justice), Tiferet (Glory/Harmony), Netzah (Triumph/Victory), Hod (Splendor/Majesty), and Yesod (Foundation). Finally, all these powers are received by and synthesized in the last Sefira, Malkhut, which releases the powers into the manifested world. Malkhut is also known as Shekhinah. It should be added that Malkhut (Sovereignty or Kingdom) is of special importance since it is the closest and direct linkage between the higher and the manifested worlds. Shekhinah, represents the synthesis of all powers of God represented in the Sefirot, and it indwells the manifested world.

I mentioned earlier that Sefirot is above the manifested world, i.e., it transcends the world. It also is immanent in the world as Shekhinah. Some Kabbalists look at Malkhut as the gate or channel through which Shekhinah, representing the synthesis of all powers, becomes the world and indwells it. Shekhina plays an important role in the practice of Kabbalah. Shekhina is considered female and represents God's presence in the world; it is most readily accessible to mankind. There is one view that Keter at the top of the Tree of Life representing the Godhead is male whereas Shekhinah is female. When an advanced practitioner of Kabbalah moves up the hierarchy of the Tree of Life, the female principle Shekhinah unites with male Keter.

It is important to point out that the qualities or powers represented by the various individual Sefiras, such as Wisdom, Kindness, Harmony, Majesty, etc., are embedded in individual human beings, and to recognize the divine source of these qualities is an important task of one's spiritual quest. Some practitioners of Kabbalah meditate on the Tree of Life made up of the Sefirot and visualize that the Tree is located in the human body (Golgwag, p. 115). According to Kabbalah the notion of a personal God, who is an object of human worship and prayer, is applicable to the Sefirot. The concept of the Sefirot has similarities with that of Ishwara-Shakti (God and His Power) of Hinduism, and I will discuss more about this in the next section.

**A Comparison of Metaphysics of Kabbalah with That of Hinduism.**

The metaphysics of Kabbalah with respect to the concepts of Ultimate Reality, God, and His relation with the phenomenal world have considerable similarities with those of Vedanta philosophy, which is one of the Hindu schools of philosophy, and I will compare these concepts. (Phenomenal world is what we perceive through our senses and also scientific instruments.) Vedanta is based on the Upanishads, Brahma Sutras, and Bhagavad Gita. The comparison will be made in general terms since despite their similarities the two different systems of metaphysics are not exactly alike.

Kabbalah's concept of Eyn Sof is very similar to that of Brahman, the Ultimate Reality of Vedanta philosophy. Brahman cannot be described and it is indeterminable. Brahman sometimes is referred to as Being and sometimes it is referred to as 'Non-Being'. The Non-Being aspect does not represent Nihil or Nothingness. The description of Brahman in negative terms, which is found in some Upanishads, is very similar to that of Eyn Sof in Kabbalah texts. Further, the Kabbalist view of Eyn Sof is panentheistic, and so is the Hindu view of Brahman. Brahman manifests as the universe and supports it as its Self, or Atman, and yet transcends the universe. In Chapter Nine of Gita this concept is referred to as the supreme secret and one verse may be quoted to present this view:

Verse 9-4. By Me, the Unmanifest Being, is all this universe pervaded. All beings are situated in Me and I do not abide in them.

Sri Aurobindo explained this verse in the book 'Essays on the Gita' as follows: "This supreme secret is the mystery of the transcendent Godhead who is all and everywhere, yet so much greater and other than the universe and all its forms that nothing here contains him, nothing expresses him really, and no language which is borrowed from the appearances of things in space and time and their relations can suggest the truth of his unimaginable being. .... All this mass of becomings always changing and in motion, all these creatures, existences, things, breathing and living forms, cannot contain him either in their sum or in their separate existence. He is not in them; it is not in them or by them that he lives, moves or has his being, — God is not the Becoming. It is they that are in him, it is they that live and move in him and draw their truth from him; they are his becomings, he is their being" (Sri Aurobindo, 1976, pp. 297 - 298).

Simultaneous with the proclamation of the transcendence of God, the Gita also makes it very clear that the transcendent (higher) reality and the phenomenal (lower) world are constituted by the same principle and that the Spirit or Self is the essence or seed of all that exist in the phenomenal world. For example, in Verse 7-10 of the Gita the Godhead (Krishna) tells His human disciple (Arjuna), "Know me to be the eternal seed of all existences". So the question that arises is how does the mutable universe of many, i.e., the phenomenal world, come out of immutable Brahman, which is one? Hindu philosophy's answer to this question is the posture of Brahman as Ishwara or God, which is the personal aspect of impersonal Brahman. Ishwara has an inherent Force, which is called Shakti. This power has consciousness and it is also referred to as 'Consciousness-Force', or 'Chit-Shakti' in Sanskrit. It is this Consciousness-Force that manifests the world, and it goes by different names in different books of Vedanta philosophy. In the Upanishads it is called Maya. The Gita calls it Para-Prakriti or Supreme Nature. This Consciousness-Force is viewed as feminine and in some Hindu spiritual practices, e.g., Tantrism, it is worshipped as the Divine Mother. It should be pointed out that Ishwara and His Shakti are not two different entities. Shakti is the power of Ishwara just as heat is the power of fire. For Hindus Ishwara-Shakti is the object of worship and prayer whereas impersonal Brahman is not. I believe that there is a strong similarity between Ishwara-Shakti of Hinduism and Sefirot of Kabbalah. I also believe that the relationship of the first Sefira of Tree of Life, which is called Keter, with the other nine Sefiras is similar to that of Ishwara and with Shakti. Keter is considered to be the Godhead of manifestation and the other Sefiras are its various powers. Shekhinah is considered to be the consort of the Godhead, Keter; similarly Shakti is considered to be the consort of Ishwara.

Shakti has many attributes or aspects. The Gita calls a divine power manifested in the world and in human beings 'Vibhuti'. Sri

Aurobindo described these powers as feminine forces in a booklet titled The Mother (Sri Aurobindo, 1974) in detail. Here I will present a few selected excerpts from his writing to show similarities between various powers and qualities of Shakti or Mahashakti, which is also called Mother, with those of Sefirot.

"The Mahashakti, the universal Mother, works out whatever is transmitted by her transcendent consciousness from the Supreme and enters into the worlds that she has made ..." (p. 29). "Many are her powers and personalities, many her emanations and Vibhutis that do her work in the universe". (p. 26). .... "Determining all that shall be in this universe and in the terrestrial evolution by what she sees and feels and pours from her, she stands there above the Gods and all her Powers and Personalities are put out in front of her for the action and she sends out emanations of them into these lower worlds to intervene, to govern, to battle and conquer, to lead and turn their cycles, to direct the total and individual lines of their forces". (pp. 32-33).

Sri Aurobindo also described four great Powers of the Mother, which are Wisdom, Strength, Harmony, and Perfection. These are manifest in individual human beings in varying degrees. In certain Hindu spiritual practices the aspirants are urged to open their human nature to these powers for transforming the lower nature to higher levels. This practice is similar to the spiritual practice of Kabbalah. The practitioners of Kabbalah meditate on the Tree of Life, which represents the Sefirot, and the various forces that comprise it.

**Concluding Remarks**

It should be clear from the discussion presented above that there are striking similarities between Kabbalah and Vedanta with regard to the concept of God. I have discussed the concept of Ultimate Reality — Eyn Sof of Kabbalah and Brahman of Hinduism. I have also discussed how according to Kabbalah the transcendent Eyn Sof manifests the world by the powers of Sefirot, and how similar this concept is to that of Ishwara-Shakti of Hinduism.

I would like to conclude this chapter by emphasizing the limitations of a comparison of the metaphysical systems of Kabbalah and Vedanta, which were developed in different times and locations. The comparison can be done only in very general terms. I also limited the scope of the chapter to only one source of Jewish mysticism, Kabbalah. A complete coverage of Jewish mysticism should include Hasidism.

## Brief Bibliography

David S., What Do Jews Believe?: The Spiritual Foundations of Judaism, Schocken Books, 1995

David, Kabbalah: The Mystic Quest in Judaism, Rowman & Littlefield Publishers, Inc., 2006

Aquila, Richard, Unpublished correspondence with the author of Schopenhauer translations, 2009

Berg, P. S., The Essential Zohar: The Source of Kabbalistic Wisdom, Bell Tower, NY, 2004

Caputo, John D., Mystical Element in Heidegger's Thought, Fordham University Press, 1986

Cohn-Sherbok, Lavinia and Dan, Judaism: A Short History, Oneworld Publications, Oxford, England, 1994

Dan, Joseph, Kabbalah: A Very Short Introduction, Oxford University Press, 2006

Gellman, Jerome, "Mysticism", The Stanford Encyclopedia of Philosophy (Spring 2014 Edition), Edward N. Zalta (ed.), URL = <http://plato.stanford.edu/archives/spr2014/entries/mysticism/>.

Goldwag, Arthur, The Beliefnet Guide to Kabbalah, Three Leaves Press, Doubleday, NY, 2005

Kurzweil, Arthur, Kabbalah for Dummies, Wiley Publishing Inc., 2007

Matt, Daniel C., The Essential Kabbalah: The Heart of Jewish Mysticism, HarperCollins Publishers, 1996

Schmidt, Gilya G., "Cleaving to God" through the Ages: An Historical Analysis of the Jewish Concept of "Devekut", Published in Mystics Quarterly, Vol. 21 # 4, December 1995, p. 103 — 120.

Scholem, Gershom, Kabbalah, A Meridian Book, Penguin Books USA Inc., 1978

Sethna, K. D., Teilhard de Chardin and Sri Aurobindo, Bharatiya Vidya Prakasan, Varanasi, India, 1973

Sri Aurobindo, The Life Divine, Sri Aurobindo Ashram, Pondicherry, India, 8th Indian Printing, June 1973

Sri Aurobindo, The Mother, Sri Aurobindo Ashram, Pondicherry, India, 1974

Sri Aurobindo, Essays on the Gita, Sri Aurobindo Ashram, Pondicherry, India, 1976

Waxman, Bob, Kabbalah Simply Stated, Paragon House, St. Paul, MN, 2004

Werblowski, Zwi R. J., "Judaism, or the Religion of Israel" in Encyclopedia of the World's Religions, Edited by R. C. Zaehner, Barnes & Noble Books, 1997

Zaehner, R. C., Evolution in Religion: A Study in Sri Aurobindo and Pierre Teilhard de Chardin, Clarendon Press, Oxford, 1971.

# Appendix:

## Place of *Bhakti* (Love and Devotion) in Sri Aurobindo's Yoga

[Translator's Remarks:

*This article was written by my late father Sri Shyama Charan Chatterji in Bengali, and it was published in August 1975 in a journal called* Sri Aurobindo Smarak Grantha *issued by Sri Aurobindo Bhavan Trust Committee of Bardhaman, West Bengal, India. Sri Saila Kumar Mitra, General Secretary of the Trust Committee, kindly gave permission to publish the article in English in* Mother India. *When translating the article I have paid attention to every word of the original article and tried not to leave out any word from the translation; however, in a few cases I reworded the sentences slightly and in that process either left out an original word and/or added a new word to make the meaning of the sentences clearer. Also, in a few cases where my father presented Sri Aurobindo's views in his own words in Bengali and I could identify Sri Aurobindo's original statements from* The Synthesis of Yoga *or* Letters on Yoga, *I have used Sri Aurobindo's words as quotations. I have abbreviated these two main sources of reference as* SY *and* LY *respectively. The book* Essays on the Gita, *from which I have used a few quotations, is abbreviated as* EG. *The original article did not have any subtitles, but in order to make the article easier to understand I have added a few subtitles and also short introductory statements to the different sections. In a few cases I have added explanatory words and quotations from Sri Aurobindo's writings and in one case from Swami Vivekananda's. The Sanskrit words used in the article are in italics, and I have presented their English synonyms in parenthesis when these words are used for the first time in the article. A list of many of these words and their English synonyms are given at the end of the article.*]

### Introduction

[*There is a wrong perception among many persons that Sri Aurobindo's yoga emphasises jnana (knowledge) and karma (work), and that bhakti (love and devotion) does not have a significant role. In fact, bhakti plays a key role in his yoga. However, Sri Aurobindo did not favour unpurified emotions, which sometimes are mistaken as expressions of true bhakti. He emphasised the need to establish quietude and peace in the mind and vital being to provide a firm foundation for true bhakti.*]

Sri Aurobindo was a great erudite person and possessed vast wisdom. He had exceptional command of several western and Indian languages. He was involved with India's independence movement for some time; however he spent a large part of his life in Pondicherry practicing yoga in solitude. Most of his books are written in English and his style of writing is a little difficult to follow. However, most of his writings in English have been translated and published in Bengali and other languages, and some of his and the Mother's advice and guidance also have been published in Bengali and other languages by Sri Aurobindo Ashram and Sri Aurobindo Society; but these are not typical religious and spiritual books. For these reasons their messages are not known very widely. Those who visit the Ashram at Pondicherry from other places observe that *sadhaks and sadhikas* (male and female practitioners of yoga) are busy in their respective pursuits and that various works of the Ashram are performed in silence. Moreover, it is seen, especially in the morning and evening, that some *sadhaks and sadhikas* are meditating near the *Samadhi* or in the Meditation Hall. [*Samadhi* is referring to the place where the bodies of Sri Aurobindo and the Mother were interred.] Sometimes there are group meditations too. There are study circles outside the Ashram where discussions are held on Sri Aurobindo's philosophy and yoga. However, one will not hear any chanting of holy names or any singing of devotional songs. Due to these reasons there are many who believe that Sri Aurobindo's yoga is comprised primarily of the yoga of knowledge and the yoga of works, and that there is no place for *bhakti* (love and devotion) in it. But this notion (that *bhakti* has no place in Sri Aurobindo's yoga) is wrong. In Sri Aurobindo's own words,

It is a misunderstanding to suppose that I am against *Bhakti* or

> against emotional *Bhakti* — which comes to the same thing, since without emotion there can be no *Bhakti*. It is rather the fact that in my writings on yoga I have given *Bhakti* the highest place. All that I have said at any time which could account for this misunderstanding was against an *unpurified* emotionalism which, according to my experience, leads to want of balance, agitated and disharmonious expression or even contrary reactions and, at its extreme, nervous disorder.... On the contrary, the deeper the emotion, the more intense the *Bhakti*, the greater is the force for realization and transformation.... It is no part of this yoga to dry up the heart; but the emotions must be turned towards the Divine.... The very basis of this yoga is *bhakti* and if one kills one's emotional being, there can be no *bhakti*. So there can be no possibility of emotion being excluded from the yoga.... Turn your emotions towards the Divine, aspire for their purification; they will then become a help on the way and no longer a cause of suffering.... Awake by your aspiration the psychic fire in the heart that burns steadily towards the Divine — that is one way to liberate and fulfill the emotional nature.... Psychic emotion is one of the most powerful helps to *sadhana* (spiritual practice). (*Letters on Yoga, Part Two*, pp. 779 -81)

In the same book Sri Aurobindo also said:

> The very object of yoga is a change of consciousness — it is by getting a new consciousness or by unveiling the hidden consciousness of the true being within and progressively manifesting and perfecting it that one gets first the contact and then the union with the Divine. *Ananda* and *Bhakti* are part of that deeper consciousness, and it is only when one lives in it and grows in it that *Ananda* and *Bhakti* can be permanent. (*LY, Part Two*, p. 785)

Thus it should be clear that the status of *bhakti* in Sri Aurobindo's yoga is very high; but what is needed at first for yoga is a quiet mind and, secondly, settled silence. Deep spiritual peace indeed is the firm foundation for lasting love and delight. That is why Sri Aurobindo did not look favourably on uncontrolled emotions. Sri Aurobindo said,

> "To bring the Divine Love and Beauty and Ananda into the world is, indeed, the whole crown and essence of our yoga. But it has always seemed to me impossible unless there comes as its support and foundation and guard the Divine Truth — what I call the supramental — and its Divine Power." (*LY, Part Two*, p. 753)

[*It may be noted that Swami Vivekananda's views about bhakti are similar to Sri Aurobindo's. He wrote,*

> *"The one great advantage of bhakti is that it is the easiest and the most natural way to reach the great divine end in view. Its great disadvantage is that in its lower forms it oftentimes degenerates into hideous fanaticism.... But this danger exists only in that stage of bhakti which is called the preparatory (Gauni). When bhakti has become ripe and has passed into that form which is called the supreme (Para), no more is there any fear of these hideous manifestations of fanaticism." (Swami Vivekananda, pp. 32, 33)*]

**Sri Aurobindo's Integral Yoga**

[*The goals of Sri Aurobindo's integral yoga include the realisation of both static and dynamic aspects of Brahman. The Divine is not only the impersonal immutable Brahman aloof from the world, He also is Ishwara, the Lord of this world, and He is immanent in the world.*

> *The object of the yoga is to enter into and be possessed by the Divine Presence and Consciousness, to love the Divine for the Divine's sake alone, to be tuned in our nature into the nature of the Divine, and in our will and works and life to be the instrument of the Divine.* (LY, Part Two, *p. 503)]*

Sri Aurobindo's yoga is called integral yoga; it strives for union with Brahman fully in all its aspects, and, therefore, its process of practice too is integral and comprehensive. In the traditional types of yoga only one aspect of God is emphasised and accordingly a single faculty of human consciousness, one power of being — mind, heart, or will — is used as the means for attaining union with God. But God represents not only existence (*sat*), consciousness (*chit*) and force (*shakti*), he is full of delight (ā*nanda*) too; and so he is called '*sachchidānanda*' (*sat-chit-ānanda)*. According to Taittiriya Upanishad the highest realisation of Brahman is as delight (*ānanda*). Brahman — the essence of existence — is described as: "*raso vai sah*" — "verily it is no other than delight" (*Taittiriya*, Verse II.7). Therefore, the question of ignoring Brahman's aspect of delight does not even arise. Existence, consciousness, and delight are not entirely separate principles; these three are intimately connected with each other. Each of these includes the other two. Although our mental process treats them separately, they are essentially same. Our basic consciousness (*chittavritti*) also is not made up exclusively by mind, or heart, or will alone. Therefore, none of these can be ignored. According to the Gita we have to find God in all his aspects. Therefore, if we want to find Brahman fully we need to approach him not only through knowledge (*jnāna*) and works (*karma*) but also through love and devotion (*bhakti*). Every portion and every aspect of our being, our thought, action and all other movements have to be dedicated to God. Meditation, or chanting of the holy name, alone is not sufficient; we must offer Him every aspect of our being and everything we do. We have to remain fully absorbed in Him. In the words of the Gita (IX-27),

> *yat karosi yat aṣnāsi yat juhoṣi dadāsi yat*
> *yat tapasyasi Kaunteya tat kuruṣva madarpaṇam.*

"Whatever you do, whatever you enjoy, whatever you sacrifice, whatever you give, whatever *tapasyā* (spiritual austerities) you practice, make it, Kaunteya (Arjuna), an offering to Me." This is a continuous *sādhanā* (practice); it requires the remembrance of and offering to God at all times — while awake, while working, while sleeping and while dreaming. As the Gita (VIII – 7) says,

*tasmāt sarveṣu kalesu mām anusmara yudhya ca*

"Therefore, remember Me at all times, and fight." The Mother too said, "Remember and offer". It is only then that His golden light will descend in every portion of our being, our entire consciousness — physical, vital, and mental — and purify and then transform them into God's divine consciousness, divine being, divine power, and divine love. In the words of Rig Veda (Hymn IX, 83-1),

*ataptatanurna tadamo aṣṇute,*

which means that he whose body has not been burnt (purified by the fire of spiritual austerities) is not able to enjoy that divine *ānanda* (delight). The verse continues to say,

*sritasa id bahantastat samasata,*

which means that only those who have become firm by being burnt in fire (of spiritual austerities) are able to contain and enjoy that *ānanda* (delight). Therefore, one should be in yoga continuously, and it is necessary to constantly remember God and offer everything to Him; this cannot be done without *bhakti.*

## The Psychic Being and Its Role

[*The psychic being according to Sri Aurobindo and the Mother is the inmost part of our consciousness and it is our true soul (purusha), which evolves from birth to birth. The psychic being is full of love and devotion for the Divine, and it plays a very important role in Sri Aurobindo's yoga.*]

Sri Aurobindo said that work, devotion, and meditation — all these three — are needed for his yoga, and that the easy way to reach God is through love, devotion, surrender and by the opening of one's psychic being; this indeed involves devotion. According to the *Katha Upanishad* (II. 1. 1.),

*Paranci khani vyatrnat svayambhus tasmāt*
*paran pasyati nantaratman:*
*Kaś cid dhira pratyag-atmanam aiksad*
*avrtta-cakṣur amṛtatvam icchān.*

"The Self-born has pierced the openings (of the senses) to face outward; therefore, one looks outward and not at the inner self. It is rarely that a wise man, desiring immortality, turns his eyes inward and sees the self within him." The seeking of pleasure by running after outside sources is not necessary. The inner self, which is the eternal source of delight, is within us, and we will possess true delight only when we will find it. In *Savitri* Sri Aurobindo wrote,

O Bliss who ever dwellst deep hid within
While men seek thee outside and never find, (p. 45)

The true individual self (*jivātman),* which transcends nature, develops its own representative in the nature part of our being, and this inmost *purusha* is what Sri Aurobindo calls psychic being (*chaitya purusha*). What is needed first is the opening of and coming in contact with the psychic being, and we need to let it be the leader of our life. There are three tasks that are emphasized in the integral yoga and these are:

> the development of the true soul or psychic being to take the place of the false soul of desire, the sublimation of human into divine love, (and) the elevation of consciousness from its mental to its spiritual and supramental plane. (*SY*, p. 144)

The Upanishads say that our inner being is hidden in the cave of our heart. According to the *Katha Upanishad*, Verse II. 3. 17,

*anguṣṭhamatrah purusha antarātmā sadā*
*jananam hṛdaye sannivistah,*

"the *purusha* who is no larger than the thumb is seated always in the hearts of men". This heart, however, is not our desire-filled, polluted, and emotional false heart. The true inner being resides

> in the true invisible heart hidden in some luminous cave of the nature: there under some infiltration of the divine Light is our soul, a silent inmost being of which few are even aware.... There dwells the little spark of the Divine . . . , and around it grows the psychic being. (*SY*, p. 141)

This psychic being should be brought out to the front with care and patience. In the *Katha Upanishad*, Verse II. 3. 17., it is said that "one must separate him (this *purusha*) with patience from one's body as one separates from a blade of grass its main fibre". This *purusha* has been derived from the delight (*ananda*) aspect of God — *sachchidananda*. That is why as the sunflower always looks at the sun, so the psychic being always turns towards the Divine.

> The most intimate character of the psychic is its pressure towards the Divine through a sacred love, joy and oneness. It is the divine love that it seeks most, it is the love of the Divine that is its spur, its goal . . . . It lifts the being towards a transcendent Ecstasy and is ready to shed all the downward pull of the world from its wings in its uprising to reach the One highest; but it calls down also this transcendent Love and Beatitude to deliver and transform this world of hatred and strife and division and darkness and jarring Ignorance. (*SY*, p. 146-147)

For these reasons it is the cave of our spiritual heart where we need to concentrate and keep in contact with the psychic being at all times. Thus it can be seen that devotion and love constitute a major limb of Sri Aurobindo's integral yoga.

**Synthesis of Different Paths**

[*Sri Aurobindo's yoga represents a synthesis of different spiritual paths including the yoga of works, yoga of knowledge, and yoga of devotion and love. This approach has similarities with that of the Gita. Sri Aurobindo explained how these paths are not mutually exclusive; in fact they are interrelated and each complements the others. In Sri*

*Aurobindo's yoga these paths work together and help transform all aspects of one's being — will, mind and heart.*]

In Sri Aurobindo's yoga there is no conflict among work, knowledge, and devotion, and this is similar to the view presented in the Gita. In the very beginning of the section on The Yoga of Divine Love of his book *The Synthesis of Yoga* Sri Aurobindo said that "will, knowledge and love are the three divine powers in human nature and the life of man" and that "the integrality of them, the union of man with God in all the three, must . . . be the foundation of an Integral Yoga." (p. 521) Life begins with force and its works, and naturally one may choose to follow the path of works, and turn all actions towards God; then one's life begins to become divine. The path of works leads also to knowledge. The Gita (IV – 33) says,

> *sarvaṁ karmakhilaṁ jñāne parisamāpyate*

"all work in its totality finds its culmination and completeness in knowledge". Sri Aurobindo explains further that in the case of a follower of the path of works

> when the will in him is made one with the divine will and the whole action of the being proceeds from the Divine and is directed towards the Divine, the union in works is perfectly accomplished. (*SY*, p. 521)

However, "the crown of this union is love; for love is the delight of conscious union with the Being in whom we live, act and move, by whom we exist". (*SY*, p. 521) Thus the path of works leads one to know the Divine and also to love and adore Him.

Some persons may choose to follow the path of knowledge to arrive at oneness with God. "Knowledge is the foundation of a constant living in the Divine." (*SY*, p. 521) But

> knowledge is not complete without works; for the Will in being also is God and not the being or its self-aware silent existence alone, and if works find their culmination in knowledge,

> knowledge also finds its fulfillment in works. (*SY*, p. 522)

Knowledge also leads to love. Actually the crown of knowledge is love.

> The vision of God brings infallibly the adoration and passionate seeking of the Divine. (*EG*, p. 310)

It is through complete knowledge that complete love arrives. In the words of the Gita (XV – 19),

> *yo mām evam asamūdho jānāti puruṣottamam;*
> *sa sarvavid bhajati māṁ sarvabhāvena bhārata.*

"He who, undeluded, thus knows Me as *Purushottama* (the Highest Person) is the knower of all and worships Me with his whole being, Bharata (Arjuna)". The Gita (VII - 17) also said, "*jnani nityayukta ekabhaktir visisyate*" — "the man of wisdom who is in constant union (with the Divine), whose *bhakti* is single-minded, excels".

Some may prefer to approach God through love. The path of love has its unique appeal. Sri Aurobindo said that knowledge is the most expansive power of consciousness, and its role is to liberate and illuminate us; but love and devotion represent the deepest and most intense principle and it indeed is the key to reach the deepest and most secret recesses of divine mystery. The Mother too said that devotion is the key for liberation. Love does not exclude knowledge. Sri Aurobindo explained further that the apparent conflict between knowledge and devotion is attributable to the limitations of lower mental and vital principles. According to the vital part of our nature (which includes emotions) mental knowledge is dry and uninteresting, whereas mental knowledge considers devotion to be merely blind emotion. But once we come in touch with our psychic being this conflict is resolved.

It is only through complete love that one can attain complete knowledge. Intellect helps us know the outer aspects of Reality, but through love we can understand the inner and deeper aspects. Paramahansa Sri Ramakrishna said that the reach of knowledge is limited to the outer quarters of the house (of God), but devotion can reach the inner quarters. In the Gita (XI – 54) it has been said,

> *bhaktyā tv ananyayā śakya aham evaṁvidhoarjuna;*
> *jñātuṁ draṣṭuṃ ca tattvena praveṣṭuṁ ca paramtapa.*

"By undistracted devotion only, Arjuna, can I be truly known and seen in this way, and be entered into, 'Oppressor of the Foe' (Arjuna)." Thus love brings true knowledge, and it also does not exclude works. Sri Aurobindo wrote that the adoration for God "is no isolated seeking of the heart, but an offering of the whole existence. Therefore it must take also the form of a sacrifice; there is a giving of all our works to the Ishwara, there is a surrender of all our active inward and outward nature to the Godhead of our adoration in its every subjective and in its every objective movement". (*EG*, p. 311)

**Spiritual Evolution and Divine Grace**

[*According to Sri Aurobindo it is the consciousness and bliss of Sachchidanada that descended and became this material world, and the hidden consciousness in matter is slowly evolving. Life (vital force) emerged from matter, and then mind evolved from life. This spiritual evolution is continuing and human consciousness is slowly ascending toward its higher supramental state. The Divine's Grace from above is ready to help an aspiring soul to ascend faster, but in order to receive the help one must surrender completely to the Divine Shakti (power). Bhakti is the driving force of this self-surrender.*]

A believer in the path of knowledge usually does not give any importance to the path of devotion considering it to be inferior; and on the other hand a devotee considers the path of knowledge to be dry and uninteresting. According to Sri Aurobindo, however, the more one knows about God, the more one's love for Him grows. Further, when love and devotion for God emerge, doing works dedicated to God becomes indispensable. Doing works for Him whom one loves is indeed an expression of love. Usually a believer of the path of knowledge considers the phenomenal world to be illusory and unreal, and so he rejects the world and seeks to merge with quality-less (*nirguna*) and impersonal Brahman. On the other hand, a devotee too rejects the world although he does not consider it to be illusory; he prefers to live in *Brindavan* (the abode of Lord Krishna), which is outside the phenomenal world, where he can remain absorbed in the delight of dwelling near God *(samipya mukti)*. But Sri Aurobindo pointed out that there is a significance of the manifestation of this world. This world is not illusory Maya. In the Gita (IV – 8) Lord Krishna said, "*dharmasamsthapanarthaya sambhabami yuge yuge*" — "I appear (in this world) from age to age for the sake of establishing righteousness". The true meaning of this establishment of righteousness is to found divine consciousness, power and delight in the world, to transform man into a divine being, and to fully express the Divine in this world. The significance of Vedantic symbol of Brahman-Wheel (*Brahman-Chakra*) is similar. The upper portion of the wheel comes down from above and enters the lower realm before it goes up again. This signifies that this world has descended from Brahman, and to ascend and return to Brahman is its destiny. According to the theory of evolution developed in the Western world, life has evolved from matter and mind has appeared from life. Sri Aurobindo accepted the western view but his view goes farther and adds that the mind of human beings cannot be the last stage of evolution. The human mind is progressing. We can see how much more advanced the mind of a modern educated person is than the mind of a wild uncivilised person (of old time). The mind of a highly spiritual person — an ascetic holy person, or a devotee of God, or a 'yogi' — is even more advanced. The *Taittiriya Upanishad* mentions a level of consciousness higher than mind and calls it *Vijnāna* (or Gnosis). Sri Aurobindo too said that mind's culmination will be in supermind, which is the mind of God. Life could emerge from matter and mind from life because they were hidden in what they emerged from. The divine consciousness with delight came down and became inconscient matter, and following the evolutionary process it is gradually emerging. Lord Krishna said in the Gita (X – 39), "*sarvabhutanam bijam aham*" — "I am the seed of all existences." That this seed will gradually grow and become a large tree is its divine destiny. Human mind, life and body are limited and incomplete, and they have to be transformed into their supramental counterparts, which lie in the higher realm. That indeed is the significance of the divine creation (manifestation), and to accomplish this task mankind has to surrender to God completely and become the channel of His power, consciousness and delight. According to the Gita (XVIII – 61), "*Ishwara sarvabhutanam hriddese Arjuna tisthati*" — "The Lord abides in the heart of all beings, Arjuna". God is dwelling in our hearts and guiding us. So when the Divine himself is our guide, our ascent to the higher realm of divine nature is certain.

Sri Aurobindo said at the very beginning of his book titled *The Mother*,

> There are two powers that alone can effect in their conjunction the great and difficult thing which is the aim of our endeavour, a fixed and unfailing aspiration that calls from below and a supreme Grace from above that answers. (p. 1)

To aspire for the Divine and to receive His Grace certainly involve devotion and love. In the Upanishads it is said,

> *nayam ātma pravachanena labhyo na medhaya,*
> *na bahuna srutena:*
> *yamevaisa vṛṇute, tena labhyas tasyaisa ātmā*
> *vivṛnute tanum svam.*

"This self can be attained neither by instruction, nor by intellectual power, nor even by much learning. Self is to be attained only by the one whom it chooses. To such a one the self reveals its own body." (*Katha* I. 2. 23., and *Mundaka* III. 2. 3.) (This refers to Divine Grace.) We already have seen that Sri Aurobindo puts considerable emphasis on Divine Grace.

Self-surrender is a major part of Sri Aurobindo's yoga. When a *sādhak* surrenders himself to God, He on His own comes to him. The aspirant then receives His Light, Power, Knowledge, and the ocean of Delight. Therefore, what is needed is complete self-surrender. There should be no demand of any kind, and we must offer to Him every aspect of our being without any reservation. This attitude and approach represent true devotion (*bhakti*).

## Nature of True Love and Devotion

[*True love for God is free of any demand and claim. It leads to unconditional self-giving and surrender to God. It is different from human love, which makes selfish demands on the beloved.*]

What is the meaning of devotion for God, or love for God? Our concept of love is based on how we love another human being. But human love is tainted; its primary goal is to fulfill selfish desire, and it is a deformed and polluted form of divine love. Human love is filled with jealousy, *abhimān* (feeling of hurt), and anger; but there is no place for these feelings in this yoga, and these are not a part of true love also. In yoga all love is directed toward God, and one should love human beings as representatives of God (who dwells in them). When one can love God with his entire being, then only is it possible for one to love a human being in the right manner. The love for the Divine is not merely a higher version of human love; it involves a different consciousness and its quality, character and movement are of another type. Sri Aurobindo made a distinction between devotion and love. He said,

> The nature of Bhakti is adoration, worship, self-offering to what is greater than oneself; the nature of love is a feeling or a seeking for closeness and union. Self-giving is the character of both; both are necessary in the yoga and each gets its full force when supported by the other. (*LY, Part Two*, p. 776)

Sri Aurobindo also said,

The true love for the Divine is a self-giving, free of demand, full of submission and surrender; it makes no claim, imposes no condition, strikes no bargain, indulges in no violences of jealousy or pride or anger — for these things are not in its composition. In return the Divine Mother also gives herself, but freely —and this represents itself in an inner giving — her presence in your mind, your vital, your physical consciousness, her power re-creating you in the divine nature, taking up all the movements of your being and directing them towards perfection and fulfillment, her love enveloping you and carrying you in its arms Godwards. (*LY, Part Two*, p. 757)

**Reconciliation of Personal and Impersonal Aspects of the Divine**

[*One philosophical issue that should be examined before concluding this article involves God as a Personal Being. There has been much debate among philosophers regarding the nature of the supreme Reality (Brahman) as to whether it is personal or impersonal, and there is a trend in modern philosophy to view Reality as being impersonal. There are also some philosophers who recognize both impersonal and personal aspects but consider the personal aspect to be lower in status than the impersonal aspect, and they choose impersonal Brahman as the goal to reach. Sri Aurobindo explained that one does not have to choose one aspect or the other since both aspects are contained in the Divine. Personality and impersonality "are one thing which we see from two opposite sides and into which we enter by two gates."* (SY, *p.553) Sri Aurobindo fully accepted the Gita's concept of Purushottama. In Sri Aurobindo's yoga a sadhaka has to surrender with love to the Divine personality — Ishwara and His Shakti — since the goal of transforming every aspect of one's being and rising to the supramental level is too difficult to accomplish by one's own effort.*]

A common believer of the path of knowledge will say that devotion and love call for an object of love, the beloved, in a personal form, and he would question if God can be limited to a human-like personality. God is not like a finite and incomplete human being with limited consciousness and polluted life. Sri Aurobindo considers Him to be an infinite Person (*Purusha*). We are overwhelmed by the impersonal vastness of the natural world, and we think that man is merely an insignificant particle of dust. But in the evolutionary process what appears later is greater than what came earlier. Life emerged from matter, and mind appeared from life. But life and mind are more powerful than matter. Similarly man with personality emerged from the impersonal world, and, thus personality is greater than impersonality. However, man's personality still is limited and incomplete, but this personality will be complete since man essentially is the son of immortal Spirit (*Amritasya Putrah*). To become immortal and infinite is his destiny, and for fulfilling this destiny man must make a conscious effort. God has been described as an infinite Being, and an infinite Person. The Upanishads refer to Brahman as 'That' (*Tat*), and also as 'He' (*Sah*) and Person (*Purusha*). In the Gita God has been described as *Purushottama* (Supreme Person) who surpasses the perishable (*kshara*) *Purusha* and is higher even than the imperishable (*akshara*) *Purusha.*

Sri Aurobindo addressed the issue of personality and impersonality of God in *The Synthesis of Yoga*, Part Three, Chapter V (p. 553). He wrote:

> Personality and impersonality....are only aspects of the Divine and both are contained in his being; they are one thing which we see from two opposite sides and into which we enter by two gates.

Thus according to his view impersonality is a quality, and is merely an aspect of God's nature, as courage is a quality of man. The existence of courage implies that there is a courageous person. Similarly if there is love, there must be a person who loves and a person who receives the love.

In *Svetāsvatara* Upanishad Brahman has been referred to as *Nirgunah*, (without qualities) as well as Guni (with qualities). The expression *Nirguna* (without qualities) does not imply that He is devoid of qualities; it really means that He is not limited by qualities. The Divine "is the *Ananta-guna*, the infinite quality and the infinite divine Personality which manifests itself through it." (*SY*, p. 561) In the Gita too the Supreme Person has been described as "*nirgunam gunabhoktr ca*" — "free from qualities yet enjoyer of qualities" (Verse XIII - 14). Sri Aurobindo wrote,

> As we ourselves are not merely a number of qualities or powers or a psychological quantity, but a being, a person who so

> expresses his nature, so is the Divine a person, a conscious Being who thus expresses his nature to us. And we can adore him through different forms of this nature, a God of righteousness, a God of love and mercy, a God of peace and purity. (*SY*, p. 560)

When God is described as 'formless', it is not meant that he is incapable of taking any form since that will limit his power. The meaning of 'formless' is that He is not limited by any form and that He can take any form, or He can also decide to take no forms. The *Svetasvatara Upanishad* (Verse IV - 3) describes Brahman as:

> You are woman. You are man. You are the youth and the maiden too. You, as an old man, walk bent with a staff. You become born and the world is full of thy faces.

In the *Katha Upanishad* (Verse I. 2. 23) too it is said that Self reveals his own body only to the one whom he chooses. Therefore, when Brahman is described as a Person (*Purusha*), no limit is imposed on Him. He is an infinite Person, and His knowledge, power, love, and all other forms of his nature are infinite and unlimited. Sri Aurobindo explained that,

> None of these are all the Divinity....He is each separately and all together. He is Vishnu, Krishna, Kali; he reveals himself to us in humanity as the Christ personality or the Buddha personality.... Again he seems to withdraw into a pure spiritual impersonality; . . . he becomes to the mind of man an indefinable, *anirdesyam*. But out of this unknowable the conscious Being, the divine Purusha, who has manifested himself here, still speaks, "This too is I; even here beyond the view of mind, I am He, the Purushottama." (*SY*, pp. 560–61)

[*In conclusion it should be reiterated that bhakti plays a major role in Sri Aurobindo's yoga. In Sri Aurobindo's words, "I have given Bhakti the highest place".* (LY, *p. 780) But he also pointed out that this bhakti is not restless and unpurified emotionalism, and that there must be settled peace in the mental and vital parts of one's being to support the emotions contained in bhakti. Aspiration, which is the first and foremost requirement for succeeding in Sri Aurobindo's yoga, represents love seeking for the Divine Mother. According to Sri Aurobindo the source of divine love for God in a person is his psychic being and the opening of this true soul hidden in his spiritual heart is of immense importance for his yoga. Further, it is through unconditional love for and complete self-surrender to the Mother, the Divine Shakti, that one is able to accomplish the goals of integral yoga of Sri Aurobindo.*]

Shyama Charan Chatterji
(Translated from Bengali by Arun Chatterjee)

## References

Sri Aurobindo, *Letters on Yoga*, Volume Two (Parts Two and Three), Sri Aurobindo Ashram Trust, Pondicherry, India, 1971 [This is abbreviated as LY in the article.]

Sri Aurobindo, *The Synthesis of Yoga*, Sri Aurobindo Ashram Trust, Pondicherry, India, 1972. [This is abbreviated as SY in the article.]

Sri Aurobindo, *Essays on the Gita*, Sri Aurobindo Ashram Trust, Pondicherry, India, 1972 [This is abbreviated as EG in the article.]

Sri Aurobindo, *Savitri*, Sri Aurobindo Ashram Trust, Pondicherry, India, 1972

Sri Aurobindo, *The Upanishads*, Sri Aurobindo Ashram Trust, Pondicherry, India, 1972

Sri Aurobindo, *The Mother*, Sri Aurobindo Ashram Trust, Pondicherry, India, 1974

Swami Vivekananda, *The Complete Works of Swami Vivekananda, Volume III*, Advaita Ashram, Calcutta 14, India, May 1973

## Sanskrit Terms and Their Meaning

*Bhakti* — devotion and love; *Guna* — qualities, or dispositions, of the nature part of one's being; *Ishwara* — the Divine as a person; *Jnana* — knowledge; *Karma* — works, action; *Purusha* — person, conscious being; *Purushottama* — supreme person; *Sadhak* and *Sadhika* — male and female practitioners of yoga; *Sadhana* — spiritual practice; *Self* — atman; *Shakti* — power.